T0318465

CULTURALLY SUSTAINING SYSTEMIC FUNCTIONAL LINGUISTICS PRAXIS

By introducing a framework for culturally sustaining Systemic Functional Linguistics (SFL) praxis, Harman, Burke and other contributing authors guide readers through a practical and analytic exploration of youth participatory work in classroom and community settings. Applying an SFL lens to critical literacy and schooling, this book articulates a vision for youth learning and civic engagement that focuses on the power of performance, spatial learning, community activism and student agency. The book offers a range of research-driven, multimodal resources and methods for teachers to encourage students' meaning-making. The authors share how teachers and community activists can interact and support diverse and multilingual youth, fostering a dynamic environment that deepens inquiry of the arts and disciplinary area of knowledge. Research in this book provides a model for collaborative engagement and community partnerships, featuring the voices of students and teachers to highlight the importance of agency and action research in supporting literacy learning and transformative inquiry. Demonstrating theoretically and practically how SFL praxis can be applied broadly and deeply in the field, this book is suitable for preservice teachers, teacher educators, graduate students and scholars in bilingual and multilingual education, literacy education and language policy.

Ruth M. Harman is Professor in the Department of Language and Literacy Education at the University of Georgia, USA.

Kevin J. Burke is Associate Professor in the Department of Language and Literacy Education at the University of Georgia, USA.

Language, Culture, and Teaching
Series Editor: Sonia Nieto

For more information about this series, please visit: https://www.routledge.com/
Language-Culture-and-Teaching-Series/book-series/LEALCTS

CULTURALLY SUSTAINING SYSTEMIC FUNCTIONAL LINGUISTICS PRAXIS

Embodied Inquiry with Multilingual Youth

Ruth M. Harman and Kevin J. Burke

Routledge
Taylor & Francis Group

NEW YORK AND LONDON

First published 2020
by Routledge
52 Vanderbilt Avenue, New York, NY 10017

and by Routledge
Park Square, Milton Park, Abingdon, Oxon, OX14 4RN

Routledge is an imprint of the Taylor & Francis Group, an informa business

© 2020 Taylor & Francis

Library of Congress Cataloging-in-Publication Data
A catalog record for this title has been requested

ISBN: 978-0-367-13979-7 (hbk)
ISBN: 978-0-367-13982-7 (pbk)
ISBN: 978-0-429-02951-6 (ebk)

Typeset in Bembo
by Cenveo® Publisher Services

CONTENTS

FIGURES

FOREWORD

The world is moving toward fostering open-solution societies. People from all walks of life are encouraged to think and plan together to apply their creativity and talents to practical solutions for social problems. As more societies face significant social issues for which effective solutions are nowhere to be found, those at the center of these problems can be the best planners, for they may be the first to see the benefits of being flexible and adaptive. Moreover, they know their environment and their fellow citizens better than anyone else.

What must guide the open-solution work are adaptability, innovative ideas and various forms of engagement. Only jointly developed group thinking toward the necessary collaborative work will provide results. Thus, the most hopeful solution is deep awareness of the need for adaptive thinking. To achieve such decentralized decision-making processes will be critical. Problem-solving by groups where everyone's idea is heard and attended to with respect has become a key move toward creating the essence of any open-solution situation.

Increasingly, we see that naturalistic social experiments such as those described in this book are creating open-solution approaches to problems. Reasons rest very much in the fact that around the world, modern economies find that the young born and raised in rural areas or small towns migrate to urban regions. Left behind are "forgotten" neighborhoods and small towns, suffering from severe changes to what long-term residents have long called home, and immigrants who find their way to such places want to call home. The major case study of this book differs from the most "forgotten" neighborhoods existing in modern economies. The "forgotten" operate in a city and also in the shadow of a world-class university intent on expansion of its real estate. To this and other similarly situated universities, migrants find their way into education, often at a great mental and cultural cost. Asked to drop their native language and leave behind their homeland culture, these newcomers struggle to adapt, succeed and find their way. In regions of the United States, African-Americans, often first-generation college students, find themselves facing issues just as severe as those faced by migrants. Housing exclusion and other policies backed by long-standing prejudice and policies of exclusion keep reminding them of "their place" or the idea that where "they should be is not here."

Remarkable about the project described in this book is the fact that the scholars, young and old, openly expressed their emotions and struggles in a variety of modes. These scholars included Blacks, Whites, and migrants from around the world. All of them worked together as they gradually found ways to make inclusion look and feel different. Perhaps most important about this story is that individuals across ages and backgrounds felt drawn to open-solution work, and by using multiple modes of representation of their emotions and ideas, individuals found themselves thinking and working with language as well as their hands and bodies toward expressing themselves. As they did so, they found that thinking together in ways that neither they nor others might have once thought possible leads to advancing creativity through innovative thinking.

In this book, we will benefit from the work of those taking part in what may be called an "experiment," because the process moved with "mindful inquiry" (Bentz & Shapiro, 1998). Essential in such inquiry is the ongoing critique of existing values and those expressed within the group through transcendence of self-interests for replacement with self-awareness. From such inquiry, social action emerges.

This book also documents the sharing of social, political and cultural differences as well as similarities. In the course of time, these emerge in one way or another for everyone in the group. Individuals realize that all of human life amounts to an ongoing process of interpreting and reinterpreting both the self and others now having to live, learn and work under new circumstances. Those taking part come to see research and self-critique as general skills that should be carried through life.

Several quite similar moves to the inquiry or research within the project laid out in this volume include: ethnography, autoethnography, Youth Participatory Action Research (YPAR) and other means of inquiry that turn the lens onto the self as well as the other and the local context in a comparative frame. What is particularly appealing about this book is the fact that tough attention goes to language, its functions and its structures. We know that what we see, how we behave and what we value and hope generally find expression first and foremost in language. Through this volume the movement of all participants toward becoming researchers lets us in on ways in which everyone involved acquired understanding, information and deep knowledge about themselves as well as others within the process.

Recall of past images feeds imagination, which in turn enables narratives. These stories yield opportunities for members of the group to debate and consider different ways of navigating the world. Doing so then pushes imagination and enables individuals to tumble in their memory both backward toward the past as well as to aspire and explore ways to move toward the future.

Open-source solutions came into being in the 1990s, along with deepening explorations of social entrepreneurship. The tying together of these two elements historically has promoted a widening of the idea of "changemakers," inspired largely by the work of Ashoka (https://www.ashoka.org), an entity created in 1981. Evolution of Ashoka over the decades has greatly benefited from the work of changemakers around the world who see issues and matters that call for shifts in the perspective toward new and different ways of making decisions, devising solutions and discerning problems and their effects on the most disenfranchised. Ashoka aligns in many ways with the goals and operations of the project described in this volume through Ashoka's fundamental belief that *all* citizens can contribute to a change in positive ways. In an "everyone is a changemaker" world, the optimal way of bringing about a change is through open-solution work organized in fluid, open, teams.

Ashoka and its many teams see the inequality that stretches across the world as profoundly painful to many individuals and also highly dysfunctional and unethical. Although individuals in this volume take a "no-attack" frame of operation to heart, what all participants intuitively know is that they are working toward removing this dysfunctionality and encouraging fundamental empathy across the university as well among policymakers and civic leaders of the region. Participants within this project gradually come to see how the various actors, within the university as well as the city, either do not see or willfully ignore ways in which immigrants, African-Americans and other disenfranchised groups are left out of true participation. Such involvement can help us move toward making up for our dereliction and ignorant actions of the past that have contributed so fully not only to climate change but also to a highly divisive world. We must now move toward making a better world—one engaged with a wide variety of skills, background experiences and hopes for a new and different way of relating to one another and to creating solutions in innovative ways. The goal is to develop empathetic and active understanding across members of groups now so divided and to hold steady a solid openness to learning both as individuals and as team members.

Both the goals of the project described in this book and those of Ashoka and other truly social entrepreneurial groups resist fitting easily into one discipline or area of academic focus, such as education or business. The work of such entities points to a sustained endeavor toward civility and democracy. The way forward rests in bringing to awareness behaviors that characterize both civility and democracy in action. Learning from and about others with openness and true sharing toward a set of changes generally gives rise to ethical awareness and recognition of the need for moral virtues. Together these rely on care, empathy, sensitive questioning, prudent examination of actions contemplated and an ongoing research or I-want-to-know perspective on the part of all participants.

Historically, the circle of concerns for humans other than those in close contact within one's own world has come from literature, especially drama, as well as from other art forms. Such can still be the case, for much of the content within these forms illustrates vividly the need for interpretation along with the realization that all who do the interpreting will not agree. Thus, deliberation, as well as a frequent return to art forms, will constantly be called for, as was the case of the project laid out in this book. From the time of Athenian theater 25 centuries past, we have known that both good and evil, aggressive and hesitant actors, as well as the seeming willfulness of climate changes may bring down even the best of ideas. But perseverance, along with continuing hope and will, today is aided by the extent of knowledge as well as by the know-how available. This CS SFL project demonstrates, in a host of ways, the extent of power available to us through information, skills and constancy. It also illustrates the growing need for all of this to be accompanied by ongoing inquiry, belief in exploring morality, and an openness to learn through new ways including arts and sciences.

With this book, one can only hope for studied attention to the processes described as well as thoughtful critique of both actions and outcomes. Much in this world needs to change, and foremost is the way we see problems and bring about solutions in concert with one another across a world of differences. In doing so, we can only learn and learn more. And is there a greater gift than our capacity as humans to do just this?

Shirley Brice Heath
Stanford University

Reference

Bentz, V. M., & Shapiro, J. (1998). *Mindful inquiry in social research.* Thousand Oaks, CA: Sage.

ACKNOWLEDGMENTS

We extend our gratitude and appreciation for all those who have supported and strengthened our praxis and our book:

To the contributing authors for their deep humanizing work with youth

To Sonia Nieto and Karen Adler for their enthusiastic support and guidance in writing this book

To the communities of Athens and South Bend who have graciously allowed us to imagine new futures and possibilities with them

To all our families and friends who support us daily in this work

1

INTRODUCTIONS: OUR BOOK AUTHORS AND CS SFL PROGRAMS

In October 2017, local community and university members gathered at the Parkside[1] Community Center adjacent to our university campus to celebrate an opening partnership between the local housing authority and our Youth Institute[2]. The maroon doors of the community center had been closed for several years, except for a summer sports program that, ironically, residents could not afford to attend. While scrubbing and painting the dusty walls of the center alongside children and adults of all ages and races, we felt it bizarre that we could see so clearly the enormous opulent buildings of the university—across the street yet, in some ways, a world away. Yet this juxtaposition of deprivation and wealth is pervasive in urban America. Ownership and dominion over urban space is a charged political and racialized process that has negative consequences on the lives and identities of underserved communities and their access to public places (Lefebvre, 1991; Soja, 1996). In other words, it is not a coincidence that the needs and interests of the Parkside subsidized housing community have been largely ignored by the city and the university even though it sits right downtown in the middle of everything. It's no stretch to think of the edifices erected around the community, massive and modern structures connected to commerce directly (hotels) and indirectly (a three-building expansion of the college of business) as encroaching both symbolically and literally. Parkside sits on valuable, and perhaps tenuous land. Similarly, many of our youth participants in the housing complex and other high-poverty neighborhoods in our small city experience life as precarious, often a dangerous terrain.

As critical literacy educators and community activists, we are called upon to engage in culturally sustaining approaches that "work within and against the systems they are a part of to disrupt or challenge ideologies of social reproduction through the literacy curriculum" (Simon & Campano, 2013, p. 22). The purpose of our book is to share our vision and enactment of what we call *Culturally Sustaining Systemic Functional Linguistics (CS SFL)* praxis. Our CS SFL programs encourage youth and adults iteratively and generatively to engage with issues connected to their world and community, with an eye toward designing innovative, equity-centered solutions to real-world problems. Simultaneously, our CS SFL programs support apprenticeship of pre-service teachers and university researchers in the field of first and second language and literacy development. Educators who participate in our programs consistently interact with students to support youth engagement in multimodal projects and to develop their capacity as multicultural participatory teachers and researchers. We see our approach aligned closely to Mirra, Garcia and Morrell (2016) and their inspirational work, as having "implications for re-imagining the nature of teaching and learning in formal and informal educational spaces" (p. 2). The hope is that we can share with readers *how* and *why* culturally sustaining SFL practices support the multilingual and civic literacy development of adolescent youth and, at the same time, the development of culturally sustaining pedagogical practices among educators.

Our work draws from social semiotic theories of multimodality, foregrounded first in the seminal work of the New London Group (1996) who framed curriculum as "a design of social purpose" (p. 73). Collier and Rowsell (2014), in a response to this focus on design and multiliteracies, call for its pedagogical applications to include playfulness and allow for "less bounded approaches to literacy that engage bodies, objects, and texts" (p. 25). Our programs encourage youth and adult participants to create and convey their insights to what they identify as significant community assets and problems in their school or neighborhood community. They achieve this through a spectrum of modalities and meaning-making resources (e.g., geographical mapping, drawing, acting and rapping). Simultaneously, the future educators are encouraged to attend to the goals, structure and enactment of curriculum design that is multimodal, participatory, playful and rigorous.

What and Who Are We?

We have been designing and implementing CS SFL programs in our region of the country since 2009. The programs have included a combined teacher education component since 2016. Our work attempts to break out of normative schooling practices and foster a vibrant permeable space with youth fully centered in the work. Over time, our relationships with the youth participants, community members and research team members deepen, although this is certainly not a linear process; we write more about the stops-and-starts of the work later in the book. Still, there are clear successes to point to in the midst of the very real difficulties that come from being in community with others. Indeed, some of our youth participants are now writers in this book or in other projects.

Our programs have involved over 30 doctoral students and an additional 100 graduate and undergraduate students working in participatory ways with youth. The individual contexts and overlapping programs upon which we elaborate throughout the book vary significantly in population, implementation and outcomes. They are, however, tied together by a shared commitment to humanizing frameworks (Paris & Winn, 2013) and CS SFL praxis. We will elaborate more on just what this praxis looks like shortly, but for now it's worth introducing the sites of the work briefly.

CS SFL Programs

Chestnut Middle School

Our oldest program developed through collaboration with teachers and youth at Chestnut Middle School, which had become nearly a predominantly Latine[3] school by 2010. When we began our collaboration at the school in 2010 and 2011, anti-immigration policies had made the lives of bilingual immigrant students highly challenging (Harman & Varga-Dobai, 2012). Draconian legislation that led to increased abrupt deportation and a ban on undocumented students from attending public universities was being proposed and passed in state legislatures in the southeast, which triggered huge anxiety among the home communities of students. Our current CS SFL work is embedded in an afterschool program at the school that puts Latine and other youth in conversation with beginning teacher educators enrolled in an initial Teaching English to Speakers of Other Languages (TESOL) certification program.

We have used Youth Participatory Action Research (YPAR) and Systemic Functional Linguistics (SFL) in a combined framework for thinking about empowering youth and revising the practices and physical space of the school. In the 12-week programs each year, a group of 15 to 18 Latine and African-American youth and 10 to 15 White, Asian and African-American adults are engaged in a range of inquiry modules. The program activities started with storytelling and Photovoice, and then move into mapping, surveying and 3D visual modeling. It culminates with a theater performance. All modules interconnect as they cumulatively develop constructs in urban planning and design.

CS SFL Summer Program

Begun first as a program that was jointly administered by the University College of Education and the school district as a way to fight summer slide and provide dynamic arts education programming for local students, this work has now shifted to our community literacy center. We use a co-researcher model, as with all of our work, putting graduate students in partnership with local youth at two sites: the Georgia Museum of Art and the Parkside Community Literacy Center (PCLC). The aim is threefold: (a) training graduate students in community-based research methods, (b) empowering youth to drive community change through reciprocal relationships with adult co-researchers and (c) providing arts encounters at the museum using spoken word, visual artmaking, performance and freewriting. Adults and youth collaborate in five inquiry modules that culminate in a community performance. The modules that require an increasingly complex and cumulative set of semiotic resources include the following: (a) digital storytelling (taking photographs and sharing stories about their lives in the city); (b) architectural modeling (building ideal and real communities through visual art and blocks); (c) fictional storytelling (reading stories that resonate with youth lives); (d) Boalian (Boal, 1979) theater role-playing and games (enacting lived experiences and discussing with the group) and (e) weekly visits to a museum to "interact" with formal art in a space beyond the school. Through these modalities, each pair of adult and youth co-researchers explore, research and represent what they want to see changed and enhanced in their communities and/or schools (e.g., in 2016, several youth members wanted to see a youth center opened in downtown). Figure 1.1 illustrates this process, showing the community plan designed by one group of youth and adult co-researchers.

The redesigning ideas for the Parkside Community Center in Figure 1.1 highlight how inside play (e.g., the couple playing tennis), the display of youth art and

FIGURE 1.1 Redesigning Parkside Community Center

an outside sports space are all part of what the group sees as essential to making the center robust and thriving for residents and visitors to the center.

Yamacraw Action Research Team

In concert with a youth activist writing center in the heart of Savannah, Georgia, we have had the good fortune to train youth writers and artists as community researchers. The work has shifted from teaching youth YPAR methods to a train-the-trainers model, where youth are now training other youth in community research methods. The work also involves identifying systemic issues affecting youth of color in the city, gathering and analyzing field data and creating policy briefs submitted to city and regional officials arguing for reform around the juvenile justice system, poverty, gentrification, food insecurity and media representation of Black and Brown youth.

Parkside Community Literacy Center

Begun as a result of the efforts of a contributing author to this volume, Jason Mizell, and a middle school participant of the CS SFL Summer Program (see Chapter 3 in this volume for details), the PCLC is located in the center of a local federally subsidized housing complex. In partnership with the housing authorities in our city and residents of the housing complex, we have succeeded to some degree— although this is always a humbling project—in creating a small community hub for intergenerational literacy and art programs and community-based research. We have invited undergraduate and graduate students to work side by side with children based on the interests and needs of our youth members. Graduate students with middle school youth have also collected oral histories, coded data and worked with a local muralist to paint a mural of their community design.

University and Medical School Partnership

The Augusta University/University of Georgia Medical School Partnership is part of a two-year community health curriculum for medical students that embeds them in local non-profit organizations with the aim of improving community health as well as developing future medical practitioners who are better oriented to assets and needs in underserved communities. The PCLC serves as a pediatric educational site for beginning medical students who do year-long residencies building community aptitude and relationships alongside their more traditional medical training. In addition, the center serves as a periodic host-site for the medical school's Mobile Medical Clinic; all of this is part of a broader understanding of literacy as holistic and intrinsically linked to community health needs and outcomes.

Who We Are: Our CS SFL Troupe

Because the writing of this book is itself a part of our culturally sustaining SFL praxis, we introduce you here, as much as we can, to our collective authoring voices—they keep expanding—developed through collaborations, struggles and relationship building over the course of roughly a decade. In other words, we do not see this work as developing from a one-person or two-person team but instead from an entanglement of spaces, artifacts, identities and stories that ideally would be represented in the form of an ever-evolving mosaic.

In this section of the chapter, we take time to allow participants in the work—across the spectrum of age and expertise—to introduce themselves and outline some of what drew them to the projects elucidated in the rest of the book. This is vital, we think, because any culturally sustaining work is, of necessity, heavily context-laden, and charged with the stories of its participants, its subjects, its co-authors and loving critics.

Edgar Chagoya

I am a Mexican immigrant from Moroleón, Guanajuato, and a senior at one of the local high schools in our small city. I am a young activist strongly involved in my community. I have participated in a range of CS SFL programs related to civic education and activism, trying to help the voices of the youth community be heard by people who have great influence over their localities, people who can often overlook youths' options, ideas and aspirations. I have received much support from my family, friends and teachers, which has allowed me to open up myself to different opportunities and projects that brought me closer to my community. In the process, I have become more interested in the role our youth gets to take in our community. Since my first experiences I have done my best to continue helping the youth in my community in different ways.

Heidi Hadley

I've always liked being around teens. They are vibrant, funny, often incisive and refreshingly honest. As a result of that, I spent several years teaching high school, spending a lot of time with high schoolers in more formal learning and literacy contexts—reading literature, writing essays and poetry. But the best moments—the most rewarding moments—were the spaces where kids brought in their own literacies—their own ways of being, and seeing, and reading the world around them. And that's probably a big part of why I do YPAR now, because the less formal learning and literacy contexts make space for kids to be ... kids, but kids who are smart, and thinking critically about the world around them and being honest about what's wrong and what's right in this world. My YPAR identity is this: I like young people. I think they are smart, so I try to hold space for their voices and their lives and their insights.

Some of my sense of why we need youth engaged in social change for equity and justice comes from my experiences as a high school English to Speakers of Other Languages (ESOL) teacher (back when it was called ESL). The students in my class wrote letters to our senator urging him to keep introducing a bill that would allow under documented youth to attend college in the United States. They did this, even though they were afraid of the repercussions for themselves and their families because they knew that education mattered for *everyone*. I've never really forgotten that group of teenagers, even though they're now fully grown adults who fill my Facebook feed with pictures of marriages, children, soccer games and family gatherings, because they had so much *hope* that the world could be a better place and that they could be a tiny part of making that change. None of them were ever able to attend college under a *DREAM ACT*, but they didn't stop dreaming.

Jason Mizell

As noted by Momaday (1978, p. vi), "Our very existence consists in our imagination of ourselves. The greatest tragedy that can befall us is to go unimagined." When I was a little boy growing up in the rural north Georgia mountains, I felt that something was missing from my life. Like most little boys growing up in Georgia, I remember watching the *Dukes of Hazzard* and *The Six Million Dollar Man*. I remember wanting to drive fast on back country roads, jump over rivers and barns and of course, outsmart the law. Many evenings I would sit riveted to the TV as Steve Austin, the six-million-dollar man, fought bad guys and saved the United States and the world from certain doom.

I wanted to be Bo Duke or Luke Duke or even better, I wanted to be Major Steve Austin. Yet, at an early age, I knew that I couldn't be any of them. I wasn't a good-looking southern boy; I wasn't White. I couldn't be a major in the U.S. Air Force; I wasn't White. I was a young Black boy growing up in poverty in a majority White county in rural northeast Georgia. I dreamt of seeing myself or someone who looked like me saving the United States on TV or driving a fast car and outwitting the police. My wish to find a hero that looked like me went unfulfilled until I entered middle school.

During my seventh-grade year, the middle school librarian changed the rules and allowed students to come to the library by themselves before school started, during breaks, after school and even during recess time. I found myself drawn to the library. I could go to the library all by myself. I could select any book that I wanted to read without a teacher standing over my shoulder telling me that my reading level was too low. I found myself drawn to a series of books based on American inventors. That was the first time that I was able to read about Black American inventors such as George Washington Carver. It was also the first time that I was able to see that Black people were and could be more than slaves or civil rights activists. Books, literacy, gave me another outlook on what my life could be.

Several years later in high school, I had the good fortune to learn with and from an outstanding English teacher, Dan Chalk. Mr. Chalk didn't let my permanent record, which held years of reports of my performance in special education reading and math classes, or his knowledge that I came from a family that lived in public housing, stop him from listening to my hopes and dreams. He nourished my love of reading and, in many ways, apprenticed me into going to college. When he took his son on college visits, he brought me along too. He helped me to see myself outside of my small rural community.

Those experiences of reading about Black people who were inventors, teachers and politicians and having a teacher who helped me to imagine myself on a college campus far from my rural community helped me to imagine my future self into existence. I didn't go unimagined.

I see it as my responsibility now to help others who have been minoritized based on their race, ethnicity, linguistic abilities, (dis)abilities, class, sexual orientation/identification and gender identity, and imagine themselves into existence. Critical literacy, the ability to see myself in what I read and to identify and critique dominant ideologies, gave me the tools to read, write and think myself into a more equitable world, a world that I could impact.

Now that I have a platform, I hold it as my responsibility to apprentice others so that working together, they can learn to read, write and imagine themselves into a more equitable future. That said, although I see myself as a mentor, I also see myself as a mentee. The young people with whom I collaborate are also my mentors. They allow me to see their worlds through their eyes. They teach me how to navigate their communities. Even though we may share a common language of Black American English, Spanish or Dominant American English, they are constantly showing me how those languages have been and need to be remixed. That remixing highlights that our culture(s) are constantly evolving to meet our current and future needs.

It is only through our (youth and adult) collaboration that we can hope to build a society that will allow everyone to see representations of themselves so that they can truly dream themselves into different kinds of existences. If the mirror that you hold up to see yourself is broken or has been whitewashed and doesn't allow you to see somewhat of a reflection of yourself, you'll not be able to see yourself, and thus, you may never come to fully exist.

Kevin J. Burke

I began my literacy research, so to speak, teaching English in a small Catholic high school in Phoenix, Arizona. My turn to activist and youth community literacy work began as a reader, through an encounter with George Dennison's

The Lives of Children (1999) and a realization that the man who'd given it to me was a conduit to a family history of community advocacy. My uncle Jack established the Alternative Schools Network in Chicago; my aunt Maria runs Illinois Action for Children, the primary advocate for high-quality early childhood education and day-care in the state; my father agitated for the founding of and increased access to local, high-quality, city colleges in Chicago; my mother headed the local school council at my elementary school in the Chicago Public School system. These men and women were early mentors in the practice of connecting community needs with educational access; they taught me, tacitly and, in some cases, quite didactically that the only way to attend to the literate needs of individuals was to figure out the ways in which communities made sense of their day-to-day lives.

Later encounters with colleagues, who were smart about the need to address the traumas of poverty and racial inequity as a necessary condition for literacy development, pushed me into thinking about how multiple affordances of art might be used to provide youth with the tools necessary for driving community change. This is a partial archive, but one that has helped me develop a conviction that I know too little to stop reading about how to be an advocate for youth, community and literacy.

Khanh Bui

Working with immigrant youth in the United States over the past years has awakened my interest in youth civic literacy work. I was initially deeply nervous entering into my first tutoring relationship with three Latine youth. At the outset, the students were shy and rarely shared with me about their family and their own situations. They just had conversations with each other in Spanish. As an English learner and international student coming from Vietnam, I was aware of—and able to empathize with, in some measure—their struggles and feelings during the process of translating their own lives in a completely new country. However, working more with them gave me the opportunity to explore their power in constructing their own identities. Their passion for learning and desire for having their voices heard altered my prior deficit assumptions. Even though they are immigrants in the United States, they do not want to hide themselves but instead they want to prove that they are competent enough to pursue a better life. First lesson, then: Educators and researchers should not underestimate youths' competence.

As posited by Gadotti (2017) when discussing Paolo Freire's global impact, "knowledge has an emancipatory function" (p. 25). Freire's approach emphasized people's ability to think critically about their situation and develop their capacity for agency, a critical consciousness. This approach helps to deepen the quality of research, while also empowering young people. In addition, when working with adults, youth gain skills such as critical thinking, knowledge and application of research methods, and opportunities to be creative and generate new insights. Second lesson, then, researchers should do research with them rather than on them. Those lessons strengthen my beliefs in working with youth to bring us all a better future.

Mariah Parker

Having found a political springboard in hip hop myself, I embrace CS SFL praxis and YPAR as an opportunity to build new springboards for youth who use hip hop to push back against marginalizing discourses and construct positive identities. The wounds left by anti-Blackness, heteropatriarchy and capitalism—wounds that I, a queer Black femme millennial, am only now learning to heal from—can also act as a powerful epistemic resource, if harnessed. Fostering civic literacy through culturally sustaining YPAR praxis is how we hand the megaphone to those in healing and those positioned for harm. We may be academics, but we cannot pretend to ourselves that our formal education is the only kind of education that matters. I embrace YPAR because of the space it creates to learn *from* youth, not just *about* them; to watch their YouTube videos, to badly imitate the new dances, to drop the beat while they bust a quick freestyle because the genius of these arts and the process of their transmission keep these kids alive, in many ways, and may give us new life, too.

Nicole Siffrinn

When I was a master's student, I volunteered to work with English learners in content-area classrooms at a rural middle school. I spent the majority of my day with a new arrival from Guatemala. Despite having a keen interest in science, he absolutely dreaded going to science class. It was too fast paced and too linguistically demanding, so he rarely attempted to participate beyond quietly completing the materials that were adapted for him. On Valentine's Day, however, the teacher had the students cut a heart out of construction paper and write a poem about the circulatory system. He was so excited that he wrote not one but three poems on the assigned topic in Spanish. At the end of the class, he proudly gave his work to the teacher, but as he walked out of the room, she promptly handed it to the ESOL instructor and said, "Here. You can have this. I can't read it anyways."

After that experience, I began questioning the support systems that were in place in and around the school and whether the instructional practices I saw and helped uphold myself actually served the diverse interests and needs of not just English learners, but all minoritized students. I grew up privileged. The curriculum was always in line with my ways of knowing and being. I still benefit from that. Many of the students I came to learn from and care about, however, did not and do not have that luxury. In working with youth, I am therefore humbled and motivated by their thoughtful and creative contributions to an institution that limits their participation in it. I am also hopeful about what Jacques Derrida described as a future to come, feeling a deeply personal and moral responsibility to create a hospitable and equitable space for the arrival of the unknown, the other, through youth-led participatory approaches.

Ruth Harman

My passion in CS SFL praxis is to support youth in conveying their insights and dreams, to become civic and artistic leaders in their communities and to break from their often minoritized subjugation in institutional discourses. I have seen firsthand how the dynamic, cultural, multimodal and linguistic repertoires of bilingual and bidialectal youth get shutdown through policing practices that scrutinize their every move. For example, at one of the schools we discuss in this book, predominantly Brown and Black children are required to line up along the walls during class breaks and move in semi-circular patterns to the next classroom without talking to or touching anyone.

I come from a divided nation, where Protestants and Catholics still fight for British recognition or Irish nationality, especially with the now-current debate about Brexit. As a woman from a postcolonial country whose native language (Irish) is not used and whose country has been split in two since 1922, I harbor an anger against social inequity and lack of language rights. In the United States, I am an immigrant but one that is positioned favorably because of my freckles and Red/White skin. I see how my skin color and class prevail over my immigrant status and feel humbled in front of my Latine and African-American middle and high school youth participants whose lives are continually threatened by new waves of racialized immigration and education policies. In recent years, I have spent time studying how to integrate Halliday's theory of social semiotics and culturally sustaining pedagogical practices and to apply this approach to teaching and community approaches that are participatory, deeply humanizing (Paris & Winn, 2013) and creative. It is forever a humbling and daunting commitment, but with our amazing community of youth, parents, educators and researchers, I try and achieve this work, an attempt which is boundless.

Conceptual Framework: CS SFL Praxis

In the last section, you heard from all the writers in this book and their different visions and reasons for working in CS SFL programs and other instantiations of YPAR. In this section, we provide a short definition of what CS

SFL praxis means to us and then explain why we feel it is needed. We would encourage you to consider when reading these sections why and if you are interested in working with youth in participatory ways and how you will achieve whatever goal emerges from or drives your work. What is your profile? What makes you want to think of work with youth differently? Was it something in your youth? How are your relationships with diverse community populations? Think of writing a short profile of your own that you keep expanding while reading this book.

In recent years, harsh immigration and language policies have created hostile environments for minoritized youth in the United States and other heterogeneous nations across the globe (Allexsaht-Snider, Buxton, & Harman, 2013). Under the Trump Government, for example, the oppressive approach to youth dreamers in this country resulted in high trauma rates for bilingual Latine youth along with their families. In the Southeast, where the co-authors of this book reside, the impact of such policies has been exacerbated by virulent punitive measures (e.g., policing and strict disciplinary regimes in school buildings) and anti-immigration practices that pretty well exclusively target students of color. In general, minoritized students of color in public schools are subjected to discipline and surveillance practices that are sharply different from the norms in dominant White suburban schools (e.g., Ferguson, 2001, 2005). The consequences of these draconian practices and policies have been shown to be highly negative for the academic, emotional and social trajectories of minoritized students (Giroux, 2009; Noguera, 2003; Winn & Behizadeh, 2011).

To counter these monoglossic perspectives, activist educators in recent years have designed and implemented resource pedagogies *with youth* that validate heterogenous cultural and linguistic repertoires and disrupt mono-cultural literacy practices of schooling. Paris (2012), for example, proposed a model of culturally sustaining pedagogy that strives to "ensure maintenance of the languages and cultures of … longstanding and newcomer communities in our classrooms" (p. 94) while taking "a critical stance toward and critical action against unequal power relations" (p. 95). Culturally sustaining action research challenges educators to validate the cultural and linguistic repertoires of students, and to support them in designing civic and rhetorical strategies that transcend narrowly defined skills in current national tests of literacy (Campano & Ghiso, 2011; Heath, 1993; Humphrey, 2006, 2010).

SFL has been increasingly used in the United States as a teaching and analytic tool to support multilingual learners in meeting academic challenges they face due to monoglossic language policies and ideologies (Gebhard & Harman, 2011). To support student understanding of the language and knowledge demands in disciplinary discourse, an SFL approach involves an overt modeling and teaching of genre and register through analysis of mentor texts, joint construction of new texts and development of a meta-language. SFL instruction, in effect, supports bilingual students in learning how to orchestrate a *functional* knowledge of the semiotic choices in disciplinary texts (Harman, 2018).

SFL praxis continues to expand its focus to include social semiotics—not only language as a meaning-making system, but all modes including color, sounds and movement that function to make meaning in a context (Potts, 2018). In other words, there is potential for the use of SFL to support—by better understanding—the language learning and literacy experiences of minoritized students who are multilingual, certainly, but also students who are not traditionally conceived as such. That is, we assert that we have an analytical lens in CS SFL that allows us to think through the ways in which multiple artistic modes of literacy can account for meaning making with youth who are marginalized because of linguistic imperialism more broadly conceived than merely, say, students traditionally dropped into the category of English as a second language learners.

Aligned with Paris (2012) and Paris and Alim (2017), we conceptualize our CS SFL approach as one that validates and sustains student cultures while also taking and supporting a critical gaze on issues of equity and power. In the case of bilingual and bidialectal students, their vast experience of language brokering in their communities (e.g., translating, representing and negotiating) provides them with sophisticated cognitive strategies that support their co-construction of transformative civic and arts inquiry projects. In order to more fully account for this language brokering, we propose a number of key points that emerge from CS SFL praxis that might be useful for researchers, teachers and youth workers going forward. The key tenets of our CS SFL praxis that we address throughout the book are as follows:

1. Culturally sustaining practices
2. SFL-informed multimodal designing and redesigning
3. Reflection literacy

Chapter 2 provides detailed descriptions of these interconnected elements that we find essential for our CS SFL praxis. However, before moving into the more theoretical explanation of these constructs, we provide you with reasons for why we have embraced this approach in our work and thereof the organization of this book.

Organization of Book

CS SFL involves a praxis that invites educators and community activists to engage in collaborative partnerships with youth and their families in ways that expand on normative literacy and language practices in school contexts. We incorporate multiple modalities and literacies to support transformative inquiry processes among youth and adults (Cope & Kalantzis, 2009). Each modal resource made available to the group may support a rich variation in meaning making and affective relationship building. Recent SFL research by the authors of this current book, for example, highlights the importance of viewing the body as a material and meaning-making resource in and of itself (Siffrinn & Harman, 2019). Also stressed in research on multimodality are the materialities and affordances of different modes for conceptual, affective and linguistic understanding. For example, Kress (2003) highlights how drawing and reading an image provides spatial depth to an inquiry in ways significantly different from verbal discourse that sequences the experience in a linear fashion. In addition, recent research on multimodality has found that learning is optimal in multilingual environments when communities avail themselves of all available linguistic, physical and cultural resources that they can choose to configure for different audiences and contexts (Martinez-Roldan, 2015; Rowe & Miller, 2016; Smith, Pacheco, & de Almeida, 2017). In other words, to support dynamic civic engagement among our participants, we advocate for multilingual meaning making, multimodal inquiry and physical engagement.

To share our work with readers, we have divided the book into several sections. Chapters 1 through 3 introduce you to the theoretical premises of the work and provide some examples of our overall design of CS SFL programs. Chapter 3, written by Jason Mizell, provides you with understanding of the lived experiences, deep insights and dreams of our youth participants in a highly conservative southern state. This chapter attests to the most important part of our work, relationship building across ages, races and class as much as that can be achieved. Chapters 4 through 6, written by Khanh Bui and Kevin Burke, Mariah Parker and Ruth Harman, and Nicole Siffrinn, respectively, focus readers on the rich affordances of the spatial and embodied modalities we use in our work. Chapter 4, explores how mapping and neighborhood walking supports our participants to turn a critical and creative lens on the vibrancy and challenges in their schools and neighborhoods. Chapters 5 and 6 provide detailed illustrations of the physical and linguistic play that our participants engage in, through immersion in theater, hip hop and other performative arts. Chapters 7 and 8, written by Heidi Hadley and Kevin Burke and Ruth Harman, respectively, attend to the robust refusals of our youth members to follow the intended curriculum we design. These refusals, consequently, allow them to take up other kinds of deeply meaningful work. Our final chapter brings together the most salient points from each chapter and offers some suggestions about applying the work in other contexts.

Inviting you as engaged scholars to be a part of this book with us, we have designed different components of the book to facilitate your reading. Importantly, the title of our book includes the word 'praxis,' a term, of course, taken from Paolo Freire (1998) who inspired so many involved in YPAR. For us, the term praxis also means that critical reflection among educators (informed by sociocultural theories of learning and retrospective inquiry of lived experiences) needs to always connect with our actual work with youth. We see praxis as highly important to our work as authors of this book and to your work as readers and potential designers of CS SFL work in classrooms, and beyond them. We provide preludes in the different sections in this book so that you can reflect on the overall purpose of the modalities and how you might apply them in your work. In addition, throughout and at the end of most chapters, we provide you with questions and topics to consider when engaging in this work as a teacher educator, a community activist or a classroom teacher.

Notes

1 All names of places and youth are pseudonyms unless we state otherwise.
2 As an intergenerational and interracial group of youth, community members, university educators and school teachers, we started CS SFL programs in 2009 to challenge the immigration and racializing discourses prevalent in our city and state.
3 We adopt Jason Mizell's use of the term Latine instead of the original term Latino in this manuscript as one way of breaking down the binary that may be produced by using the term. Latino generally implies that one is either male (Latino) or female (Latina). Latine is used to express that within the community of those who identify culturally, linguistically or otherwise with those who reside in Latin America there exist numerous ways of identifying other than as simply male or female. Some Spanish speakers in Latin America now use this term instead of Latinx as it is pronounceable in Spanish, whereas Latinx isn't.

References

Allexsaht-Snider, M., Buxton, C., & Harman, R. (2013). Challenging anti-immigration discourses in school and community contexts. *International Journal of Multicultural Education*, *14*(2), 1–9.

Boal, A. (1979). *Theater of the oppressed*. New York, NY: Theater Communications Group.

Burke, K. J., Harman, R., Hadley, H. L., & Mizell, J. D. (2018). "I almost feel like I didn't get the chance to really begin": Challenges and opportunities in a critical, project-based clinical experience. *New Educator*, *14*(3), 212–230.

Campano, G., & Ghiso, M. P. (2011). Immigrant students as cosmopolitan intellectuals. In P. Coates, P. Enciso, C. Jenkins, & S. Wolf (Eds.) *Handbook on research on children's and young adult literature* (pp. 164–176). Mahwah, NJ: Erlbaum.

Collier, D. R., & Rowsell, J. (2014). A Room with a View: Revisiting the multiliteracies manifesto, twenty years on. *Fremdsprachen Lehren und Lernen*, *43*(2), 12–28.

Cope, B., & Kalantzis, K. (2009). Multiliteracies: New literacies, new learning. *Pedagogies: An International Journal*, *4*, 164–195.

Dennison, G. (1999). *The lives of children: The story of the first street school*. Portsmouth, NH: Boynton/Cook Publishers.

Ferguson, A. A. (2001). *Bad boys: Public schools in the making of black masculinity.* Ann Arbor, MI: University of Michigan Press.

Ferguson, A. A. (2005). From bad boys: Public schools in the making of black male masculinity. In E. R. Brown, & K. J. Saltman (Eds.) *The critical middle school reader* (pp. 311–328). New York, NY: Routledge.

Freire, P. (1998). *Teachers as cultural workers: Letters to those who dare to teach* (D. Macedo, D. Koike, & A. Oliveira, Trans.). Boulder, CO: Westview Press.

Gadotti, M. (2017). The global impact of Freire's pedagogy. *New Directions for Evaluation, 2017*(155), 17–30.

Gebhard, M., & Harman, R. (2011). Reconsidering genre theory in K-12 schools: A response to school reform in the United States. *Special Edition of Journal of Second Language Writing, 20*(1), 45–55.

Giroux, H. A. (2009). *Youth in a suspect society.* New York, NY: Palgrave Macmillan.

Harman, R. (Ed.). (2018). *Bilingual learners and social equity: Critical take(s) on systemic functional linguistics.* London, UK: Springer.

Harman, R., & Varga-Dobai, K. (2012). Critical performative pedagogy: Emergent bilingual learners challenge local immigration issues. *International Journal of Multicultural Education, 14*(2), 1–17.

Heath, S. B. (1993). Inner-city life through drama: Imagining the language classroom. *TESOL Quarterly, 27*(2), 177–192.

Humphrey, S. (2006). Getting the reader on side: Exploring adolescent online political discourse. *E–Learning, 3*(2), 143–157.

Humphrey, S. (2010). Modelling social affiliation and genre in the civic domain. In A. Mahboob, & N. Knight (Eds.) *Appliable linguistics* (pp. 76–91). London, UK: Continuum.

Kress, G. (2003). *Literacy in the new media age.* London & New York: Routledge.

Lefebvre, H. (1991). *The production of space.* Malden, MA: Blackwell.

Martinez-Roldan, C. M. (2015). Translanguaging practices as mobilization of linguistic resources in Spanish/English bilingual after-school program: An analysis of contradictions. *International Multilingual Research Journal, 9*, 43–58.

Mirra, N., Garcia, A., & Morrell, E. (2016). *Doing youth participatory action research: A methodological handbook for researchers, educators, and youth.* New York, NY: Routledge.

Momaday, N. S. (1978). Indian voices. In G. R. Vizenor (Ed.) *Wordarrows: Indians and whites in the new fur trade* (p. vi). Minneapolis, MN: University of Minnesota Press.

New London Group. (1996). A pedagogy of multiliteracies: Designing social futures. *Harvard Educational Review, 66*(1), 60–92.

Noguera, P. (2003). The trouble with black boys: The role and influence of environmental and cultural factors on the academic performance of African American males. *Urban Education, 38*(4), 431–459.

Paris, D. (2012). Culturally sustaining pedagogy: A needed change in stance, terminology, and practice. *Educational Researcher, 41*(3), 93–97.

Paris, D., & Alim, H. S. (2017). *Culturally sustaining pedagogies: Teaching and learning for justice in a changing world.* New York, NY: Teachers College Press.

Paris, D., & Winn, M. T. (2013). *Humanizing research: Decolonizing qualitative inquiry with youth and communities.* Thousand Oaks, CA: SAGE.

Potts, D. (2018). Critical praxis, design and reflection literacy: A lesson in multimodality. In R. Harman (Ed.) *Bilingual learners and social equity: Critical take(s) on systemic functional linguistics* (pp. 201–224). London, UK: Springer.

Rowe, D. W., & Miller, M. E. (2016). Designing for diverse classrooms: Using iPads and digital cameras to compose eBooks with emergent bilingual/biliterate four-year-olds. *Journal of Early Childhood Literacy*, *16*, 425–472.

Siffrinn, N., & Harman, R. (2019). Toward an embodied systemic functional linguistics. *TESOL Quarterly*. Retrieved October 2019, from https://doi.org/10.1002/tesq.516.

Simon, R., & G. Campano. (2013). Activist literacies: Teacher research as resistance to the 'normal curve.' *Journal of Language and Literacy Education*, *9*(1), 21–39.

Smith, B., Pacheco, M., & de Almeida, R. (2017). Multimodal codemeshing: Bilingual adolescents' processes composing across modes and languages. *Journal of Second Language Writing*, *36*, 6–22.

Soja, E. (1996). *Thirdspace: Journeys to Los Angeles and other real-and-imagined places*. Cambridge, UK: Blackwell Publishers.

Winn, M. T., & Behizadeh, N. (2011). The right to be literate: Literacy, education, and the school-to-prison pipeline. *Review of Research in Education*, *35*(1), 147–173.

2

CS SFL PRAXIS WITH MULTILINGUAL[1] YOUTH: WHAT ON EARTH DOES *THAT* MEAN?

In 2013 I came here, but before that I always felt supported by my family and my community back in Mexico. I always felt confident and it felt like I had good communication skills, and after my family decided to come to the United States I had a big struggle with that. I lost confidence, I lost my communication, especially my communication, as I had no English vocabulary, probably I just knew the colors, the numbers and some animals. I clearly didn't take any English classes in any way before; I was going blindly into a new environment, in which I had to adapt. And that was really hard for me, as I just struggled. In my struggle I noticed that I and many other students out there, who have a great potential, are not able to achieve their goals yet because they have not been given the resources necessary to actually step up (Edgar Chagoya, Graduate North American Systemic Functional Linguistics Conference, 2017).[2]

Edgar, one of our amazing youth members and a contributing writer in this book, believed our *Culturally Sustaining Systemic Functional Linguistics (CS SFL)* youth programs could support him and his peers in building up their rhetorical, civic and academic repertoires within their new cultural context. He was much more hesitant about the purpose and success of high school testing practices. He stated that in his observation of other immigrant and U.S. students even those "who know perfect English struggle with the material that we have to, or actually teachers have to go through. It's just extensive they have to go through all this material, break it down even further." Importantly, Edgar saw current school practices as not the fault of teachers but the fault of a flawed state and federal system that puts undue pressure on teachers to cover vast amounts of material in a compressed time frame. The result of these practices, however, is that multilingual youth like Edgar are left feeling isolated in institutions that should be supporting their dynamic disciplinary development (Gebhard, 2019). As Gebhard states, this marginalization happens increasingly "in the context of globalization, where students' linguistic and cultural resources meet, collide, and often go unrecognized as having value by other students, teachers, and administrators" (p. 28). This trend toward deficit teaching/learning practices in institutional spaces is felt deeply by insightful young men such as Edgar and our other youth participants.

To support Edgar, his peers and his teachers, we developed our contextualized CS SFL approach to working with youth in after school and community centers. We try to put youth voices and interests at the center of the work. We often flounder, fall on our faces and get up again in this difficult work as Winn and Winn (2016) explain about their Youth Participatory Action Research (YPAR):

> We, like many social justice and value-centered scholars, grapple with the complexities and tensions of conducting YPAR with youth who are routinely exposed to a standardized curriculum with few opportunities to think, write, engage, challenge and discuss critically socially and culturally relevant issues that impact their daily lives. (p. 112)

In this chapter, we explain the theoretical underpinnings of our combined CS SFL approach to community problem-solving with youth. In the concluding section of this chapter, we pose some questions that might be useful if you are interested in using a similar approach in your classroom or community work.

Our Theoretical Framework: CS SFL Praxis

Aligned with recent educational and sociological research, our CS SFL praxis highlights the power of performance, community action, visual artmaking and multilingual meaning making to position youth as civic agents of change and artistic remixers of knowledge (Paris, 2012; Paris & Alim, 2017). Informed by Halliday's theory of SFL, our approach complements recent contributions in the field of YPAR and civic engagement. We place special attention on designing curriculum that fosters creative remixing processes of youth and adult allies engaged in deep relational, embodied and cognitive work (Humphrey, 2010). The key tenets of our CS SFL praxis addressed in this chapter are as follows:

1. Culturally sustaining pedagogy (CSP)
2. SFL as language variation equity
3. Designing and remixing in multiple modalities
4. Reflection literacy
5. Adults as co-researchers

Culturally Sustaining Pedagogy

Paris and Alim (2017) posit that "culturally sustaining pedagogy exists wherever education sustains the lifeways of communities who have been and continue to be damaged and erased through schooling" (p. 1). The call in their work for restorative justice is challenging to follow, but important to attempt to implement. Indeed, CSP only exists when educators and youth activists see minoritized youth and their communities as the dynamic fulcrum for all curriculum design and community problem-solving. By centering communities of color and their funds of knowledge (González, Moll, & Amanti, 2005), the approach works to destabilize the White gaze (Yancy, 2008) that for centuries has been the measuring stick by which the knowledges of communities of color have been judged. Our CS SFL participatory approach attempts to redirect and upend that gaze by recognizing, valuing and explicitly seeking the participation of those who are insiders to minoritized communities. It is within a dynamic space of multilingual and multi-semiotic meaning making that youth and adults remix, recreate, extend and combine their home knowledges, wider community and school sanctioned knowledges to create something that will serve to meet their current and possible future linguistic, cultural and political realities.

As an example of this CSP approach in our work, our afterschool programs in Spring 2016 and 2017 were designed to support participants in using whatever languages, media and modalities (e.g., drawing, hip hop, dancing, acting) that they felt drawn to using and developing. Encouraged by the multilingual nature of the space, intergenerational and interracial small groups shared stories about what they liked and disliked about their neighborhood using Spanish, Mandarin-Chinese and varieties of English that supported all members to move in and out of whatever linguistic resources felt most comfortable to them. As illustrated in Figure 2.1, they shared about their communities in whatever language and mode they felt like using.

In addition, although they participated in a sequenced range of artistic activities including hip hop and theatrical improvisation, youth members brought divergent epistemologies and insights about what needed to be changed or added in their community and schools. It was the work of the adults to respect, make room for and follow their insightful choices. Beyond this, the group work moved to a final argumentation to be presented to school administrators or city council members that needed to be sophisticated, innovative and compelling. Academic, social and cultural networks of knowledge were incorporated in the approach.

SFL: Language Variation Equity

Over the past 30 years, SFL has been used as a teaching and analytic tool in supporting advanced proficiency in first and second language literacy from elementary to higher education contexts (Schleppegrell, 2013). Less research has

FIGURE 2.1 Building Community

conceptualized how SFL can be used to develop successful openings to students' multiliteracies *including* explicit incorporation and validation of their cultural and linguistic repertoires *along with* development of their critical language awareness. Yet these culturally sustaining approaches (Harman & Khote, 2018; Paris, 2012) afford learners with pivotal resources to appropriate and challenge dominant knowledge domains (Hasan, 2011).

One of Halliday's reasons for developing SFL in the 1950s was to counteract virulent linguicism on the part of language majority speakers (Christie, 2007). Indeed, from early in his career (e.g., Halliday, McIntosh, & Strevens, 1964), Halliday saw institutional bias toward certain dialects and hybrid language practices as directly informed by a societal desire to marginalize the cultural identities of societal subgroups. Similarly, Hasan (1996) stated, "We not only use language to shape reality, but we use it also to defend that reality, against anyone whose alternative values might threaten ours" (p. 34). To grapple with these ideological realities, SFL as an educational theory and praxis encourages learners and teachers to see and use language as a pliable configuration of choices that can support and disrupt institutional and social meaning making in a range of contexts. For example, collaborative analysis of the school language of science can lead to discussions of how school knowledge is generated through systematic use of nominalizations (e.g., turning verbs into nouns) and passive voice. The metalinguistic awareness of how science knowledge is construed supports learners in both appropriating the resources for their own needs and challenging this type of authoritarian discourse that hides agency of say, climate change and pollution (Sharma & Buxton, 2018).

When discussing how language is used to make meaning in a context of a given situation, Halliday and Matthiessen (2004) identified three situational variables—*field, tenor and mode*. When we meet our friends in a local pub after the summer holidays, for example, we usually have various topics to discuss (*the field*), a relationship with the people (*the tenor*) and a face-to-face discourse to enact (*the mode*). These three variables are realized simultaneously in the *semiotic register* through an *ideational* representation of reality (e.g., use of concrete nouns and verbs to represent or reflect on our understanding), an *interpersonal relationship* with the audience and subject matter (e.g., use of gestures, intonation, verbal appraisal), and a *textual* organization of the text (e.g., face-to-face versus written channel). Register, in sum, is defined as a "configuration of meanings that are typically associated with a particular situational configuration of field, tenor, and mode" (Halliday & Hasan, 1989, p. 39). Our friends, at the pub, would be more than surprised if we showed up with a power point describing cause and effects of soil contamination on our holiday site or if we stood up on the top of the table and began orating a talk about leisure time. When supporting youth and adult participants in our CS SFL praxis, we need to think about the wealth of registers, modalities and audiences that we can make available to participants. In that way, they can generate new knowledge through use of an expanded set of semiotic and material resources. Too often, on the other hand, school means sitting passively all day in one desk with only one audience of teachers and classmates and the expectation that one will produce state-sanctioned knowledge in mostly narrowly prescribed modes of address.

In our multilingual contexts, our CS SFL approach supports meaning making that emerges from use of as many available meaning making repertoires as possible (e.g., dialects, languages, range of modes). For example, if a group of students is multilingual, they may shift to Spanish from English to highlight or invoke ideational, interpersonal or textual meanings in the same register or to switch between registers (Matthiessen, 2018). They may also use images, gestures and movement to convey and expand on their insights. Each of these resources supports a rich embodied community practice where deep meaning making is optimized. The instructional approach validates and supports multilingual learners in constructing meaning through dynamic interweaving of all available linguistic and semiotic repertoires (García, 2009). In our CS SFL praxis, therefore, we encourage use of whatever languages and dialects and knowledge that are privileged by youth and adult members, including in the past, varieties of English, Spanish and Chinese.

SFL Curriculum Design

In CS SFL praxis, we see multilingual and multimodal interaction (e.g., via drawing, discussion, writing, dancing) as supporting youth in generating understandings of a disciplinary concept. In other words, our framework puts as much emphasis on multimodal, multilingual and participatory engagement as individual production because different modalities (e.g., visual, movement, verbal) and epistemologies (understandings of concepts that youth bring to our work) mediate conceptual understandings in different but complementary ways. This approach is informed by Vygotsky's (1978) sociocultural understanding of learning as always mediated through social, semiotic and physical engagement. Our multimodal and multilingual interactions with others through language and other semiotic and material systems support collaborative and cognitive development.

In this vein, an SFL-informed approach to instruction supports close attention to the resources (e.g., multimodal graphs, written reports, linguistic patterns) that make meaning in dominant school subjects such as physics, biology and other subject areas and in civic contexts such as public argumentation and urban design (Gebhard, 2019; Harman, 2018). For example, in the SFL-informed teaching/learning cycle (TLC), the first phase, a *deconstruction phase*, involves activating learners' understanding of the subject matter or "field" and discussion of the modalities that the students will use in enacting disciplinary knowledge (e.g., 3D visual model of a building, argumentation based on design in urban planning). In the second stage, *joint construction*, students are encouraged to write, talk and embody the subject area collaboratively through active participation of peers and teacher. In the final stage of the cycle, students apply their new understandings to a new task in writing about or enacting a scientific or civic principle. In other words, through use of a deliberately sequenced set of stages, multilingual learners are supported in co-constructing knowledge in academically, creative ways.

Importantly, our CS SFL approach sees embodiment (i.e., use of the whole or parts of the body in working around and with visual, verbal and movement texts) as playing a key role in the cognitive, linguistic and emotional development of youth (see Siffrinn & Harman, 2019). Our adaptation of the TLC encourages use of two planes of learning, one that focuses on discursive understanding of disciplinary practices (e.g., talk, modeling of writing) and one that focuses on embodied learning (e.g., physical, visual modalities). This pedagogical frame incorporates material, embodied and multilingual repertoires in the learning process. CS SFL practitioners, in other words, perceive instructional scaffolding as necessarily designed at both a macro level and a contingent level to support students in gaining confidence in shifting among registers, modes and genres in embodied and discursive ways (Hammond & Gibbons, 2005; Gibbons, 2006; Schleppegrell & Moore, 2018). In this way, SFL-based instruction promotes register variation and semiotic meta awareness that can lead to critical reflection and creative remixing of available resources.

Multimodal Designing and Remixing

A key tenet of our work is to support youth in using and expanding their semiotic repertoires through engagement in multiple modalities (e.g., drawing, performing, rapping). Our pedagogical framework draws from social semiotic theories of multimodality, foregrounded most prominently in the work of the New London Group (NLG) (1996). NLG framed curriculum as "a design of social purpose" (p. 73). The approach challenges educators to take up a metalanguage of multiliteracies to attend to the goals, structure and enactment of curriculum design. Within this pedagogy, design is conceptualized as the process in which resources and patterns from multiple modes and media are made available so learners can creatively remix them to make new meaning for their own social purposes. According to Hasan (2011), such a contribution of new knowledge to our society is a key civic right of all citizens. Thereby, the focus on design thinking and action in CS SFL aims to be transformative.

In contemporary 21st century discourse, generatively moving from one mode to another (called transmediation by Semali, 2002) is an important resource for all learners, given that contemporary discourse involves use of multiple modes and communication channels that have co-evolved with the increasing complexity of disciplinary and community knowledge. For example, Kress (2003) discussed the prominence of visual literacy in 21st century social discourse. The visual is but one example of a range of representational and communicational modes, such as gesture, movement, music and spatial configuration, which are frequently interwoven in the meaning-making process (Cimasko & Shin, 2017). Processes of transmediation support learners in constructing analogous meanings in sign systems different from the one in which the meaning was originally encoded. This process of moving across modes and registers supports youth in deepening their abstract thought, semiotic awareness and dynamic knowledge generation (Harman & Shin, 2018).

In different but complementary ways, recent language and literacy literature also supports the value of community design thinking to engage youth in developing civic agency. Design thinking about community is a methodology based on the work of Herbert Simon (1996), used to solve complex local problems and find innovative solutions integral to the desires and insights of the people involved. From this perspective, designers engage in innovative thinking about contemporary structures and practices so that they can remix available resources to create better and preferred ones. For instance, youth of color in urban communities have used design-based informal learning processes to: redesign a local park and advocate for community support through official governmental channels (Burke, Greene, & McKenna, 2016; Greene, Burke, & McKenna, 2015); fight pushout related to gentrification (Kinloch, 2010); and compose and broadcast youth community concerns through radio production (Green, 2016). Ultimately, through this work, youth are dynamic civic agents of community change while co-constructing knowledge of urban planning, environment and design.

By incorporating design instruction and thinking into our CS SFL praxis, we position youth and their adult allies as community agents of change and

FIGURE 2.2 Multimodal Expression

as multimodal designers of meaning in a range of modalities (visual, haptic [i.e., use of hands], embodied). In other words, youth are apprenticed into thinking about their communities in innovative ways through immersion in a carefully sequenced set of curricular modules that are orchestrated so they move from more everyday knowledge to collaborative co-construction of complex arguments that can be conveyed to community leaders or school administrators. Figure 2.2 shows one youth participant designing a youth space for her school through engagement in a range of modalities and interactions with co-researchers.

Reflection Literacy

Hasan (1996) discussed how reflection literacy supports teachers and students in seeing language as a pliable resource, used to enable configurations of meaning for different contexts and purposes. Through a shared metalanguage and discussion of language in literature or social media, even small children can play with and investigate how particular patterns of semiotic resources construct highly valued or less valued characters or settings (Williams, 2000). Importantly, critical language awareness for Hasan emerges from close semiotic analysis of texts rather than from interactions with texts that remain in one mode, for instance from discussions of the content of a text. Hasan (1996, 2011) also stresses the importance of creativity and redesign of available modes in reflection literacy. Our aim in CS SFL is to support youth and their adult allies in reflecting on the social structures, resources and practices that can support and impede them from thriving in school and in their neighborhood contexts. We also aim to support our participants in taking full advantage of the pliability of semiotic choices to make meaning in compelling ways for social, political and academic purposes. For adult participants, involvement in this work supports their understanding of the affordances of multimodal and multilingual resources that they can integrate into their curriculum design for their own classrooms (Harman, Siffrinn, Mizell, & Bui, in press).

Overall, our CS SFL praxis includes a focus on design as a social semiotic approach to participatory work with youth operationalized through reflective, embodied and multi-semiotic processes.

Adults as co-researchers

Our CS SFL programs always include adults, especially pre-service teachers, as integral members. Echoing Paris and Alim (2017), our aim is to place minoritized youth at the center of this intergenerational and interracial community of practice with adults by incorporating their dreams, insights and knowledge into the inquiry processes and importantly through their development of close relationships and collaborative research with adult participants. In learning to take a decentered role in the teaching/learning cycle with youth, teachers develop a heightened understanding of the social and institutional inequities that their students face. Abu El-Haj and Rubin (2009) found that after immersion in YPAR, novice teachers developed pedagogical designs more aligned with student needs and interests. In a more recent study, Rubin, Abu El-Haj, Graham, and Clay (2016) found that pre-service teachers engaged in YPAR were more likely to develop a social justice pedagogy "that goes beyond providing an equitable civic education, instead aiming to create transformative civic learning experiences that help students to interpret, resist and creatively address the forces that affect their lives" (p. 434). Overall, the CS SFL praxis compels us as educators and researchers in grappling with and reflecting on our tendency to control youth learning processes in ways that stifle their vibrant insights and reinforce normative institutional practices.

In a combined program such as ours, the multimodal arts-based approach supports youth *and* adults as they engage in deep interactions around social equity and imagined futures that disrupt normative school discourses. It also supports new teachers in seeing the importance of multimodality and dynamic theories of meaning making and the arts as a basis for youth-oriented curriculum. Vicky Hale, one of our adult participants, a veteran writing teacher but new to SFL and multimodality, stated the following when asked what she felt she had learned most from being involved in the CS SFL program:

> Like, just like I did the backwards curriculum.[3] But if you…um, if you taught how to argue something, or how to defend something, or how to stand up for something, uh, and you play it out or you use the different multimodality, or the photovoice, or whatever, and then you work backwards to writing it, and you use the functional aspect of it, to me it just makes so much sense. (Interview, April 2017)

Through use of a range of modes and multi-semiotic resources, our objective is for educators to develop critical semiotic and knowledge awareness.

We also believe that classroom discourse needs to be designed in ways that support co-construction and scaffolding of knowledge *with* youth. Herbel-Eisenmann, Drake, and Cirillo (2009), for example, provide mathematics teachers with discourse strategy training, which supports them in thinking about how to change their discourse to support register shifting through different uses of sign systems and modalities (e.g., algebraic computing, multimodal graphing, verbal reasoning). For similar reasons, pre-service teachers enrolled in our programs learn SFL and interactional theories of discourse analysis and use this knowledge to expand and reflect on their multilingual and multimodal interactions with youth. Some participants begin to see that they do not need to speak the languages of our youth (although of course this helps immensely) to support full negotiation of all linguistic resources in meaning making. As Herbel-Eisenmann, Drake, and Cirillo state, the use of SFL in our work "assumes that if students do not learn to use particular kinds of language with meaning, it is because they have had too few opportunities to use that language meaningfully in relevant contexts" (p. 185). Hence, supporting pre-service teachers in gaining knowledge of how to move across registers, languages and modes with youth in culturally sustaining ways is a necessary part of our work.

Primarily, our work with youth and pre-service teachers exists to facilitate all of us in "teaching [or learning] against the grain" (Cochran-Smith, 2001, p. 3). The partnerships among university researchers, pre-service teachers and youth are strategically developed to support all participants in interacting closely and in multi-semiotic ways around issues of social inequity and imagined social change (e.g., lack of public transportation and youth centers in our impoverished city). Only through systematic and collaborative work such as culturally sustaining approaches to engagement with youth, can we start to dismantle the tall cold walls of neoliberal institutions.

CS SFL Design Curriculum

We agree with Lee, Quinn, and Valdés (2013) that the demands for learners in the Next Generation Science Standards, which focus on embodied inquiry practices, represent a highly positive shift for multilingual learners in classrooms. Through the new focus on embodied learning and complex creative design, learners are encouraged to create multimedia designs of new concepts and engage in language rich interactions with others. However, what we caution against in such work is the assumption that engagement in embodied practices automatically produces the complex multimodal, oral and written discourses that dominant policy makers and teachers expect to emerge from classroom instruction (Buxton et al., 2019). In other words, we conceptualize our embodied work with youth as not only using multimodality as a key component. Instead, the embodied and discursive work is organized in deliberately sequenced ways to support cumulative and collaborative knowledge development. In this way, multilingual youth are supported in deepening their academic, semiotic and emotional engagement in knowledge generation over time.

When designing curriculum for CS SFL, we begin by thinking creatively about what modes (e.g., speaking, drawing, mapping, writing) can support the community focus of our youth (e.g., sustainability, spatial reconfigurations, food equity) and how our use of these modes will provide participants with a widening range of semiotic resources to support their creative remixing of existent designs and systems. Through deliberate orchestration of the curriculum modules (e.g., sequences of activities that move from more every day to more reflective domains over time), we aim to support our participants in recognizing (Bezemer & Kress, 2016) and appropriating available designs and resources for their own remixing purposes.

Discussing designs for and with youth in our CS SFL praxis involves sensitizing them to available resources and their attendant affordances, including the value of their own linguistic resources and the cultural repertoires that they, individually and collectively, bring to the mix (Potts, 2018). For example, in our 2017 program, CS SFL participants engaged in mapping their school and then moved to building with blocks and paper a design of a new building or other resource they wanted to see added to the school (e.g., running track, lounge, shop). Finally, youth were asked to argue for their new structure in a theater event, where they used argumentation, design displays and persuasive embodied language to convince school administrators of the saliency of their project.

It is also true, however, that our planning—both with and in the absence of youth—often produces a conflict between the ways in which we conceptualize the utility of a given mode for the conveyance of meaning in a situation and the knowledges and desires that our youth members bring to the table. As we discuss later in this book, often enough, youth find ways to resist/reconceptualize the modes we present as ideal (Burke, Harman, Hadley, & Mizell, 2018). This, we think, is not failure as much as engagement in productive thinking. That the youth differently channel their efforts through various modes (e.g., refusing to write poetry, but choosing to illustrate their thinking in verbal performance and visual renderings with paint) is a sign of the development of youth agency, certainly, and is a manifestation of voice and efficacy that was always already present (see Tuck & Yang, 2014) and often enough merely lacking the artistic resources and space for articulation.

Examples of Designing and Remixing

Overall, the purpose of CS SFL praxis is to ensure that youth knowledges are validated and integrated into co-construction of community problem-solving. Secondly, the objective is that youth and their adult partners move beyond reproduction of knowledge into creative remixing for their own purposes (Hasan, 2011; Paris & Alim, 2017). In our community projects, youth and adult allies remix all available resources, ranging from building blocks to GPS mapping devices, to make meaning for multiple purposes and audiences. In one project, for example, adolescents used photovoice, poetry and shared personal narratives to research aspects of their lived experiences and subsequently to perform their stories for a city-wide audience. Their stories helped to deepen community understanding of the rich lives of the multilingual youth in our area, and positioned youth as agentive civic participants (Harman, Johnson, & Chagoya, 2016). Edgar, for example, was a newcomer to the United States when we embarked on the storytelling project. His investment in the artistic processes over six months supported him in gaining confidence, in supporting other multilingual learners who were isolated in his school and in becoming a youth leader in our CS SFL program and other organizations in our city. At 14 years of age, Edgar (Harman, Johnson, & Chagoya, 2016) stated:

> These projects are important to kids like me who need to learn English and have another way to be back at school to make friends and know people who can help us. We need people to open their minds, to help us so that we can learn and grow. (p. 229)

The artistic remixing of lived experiences, linguistic resources (he told his story in Spanish) and multimodal artefacts in Edgar's first CS SFL program, as a complete newcomer to the United States and middle school, supported him in conveying deeper understandings and seeing how his classmates were understanding their new lives as well.

As Bode (2019) stated, "art and design Education creates intertwining branches of critical global citizenship and contemporary contexts that can bring tangible, recognizable motivation for change among communities" (p. 1). We have seen transformation take place when youth become the full center of our work and when adults support them in creatively and critically engaging with the world around them. Through the generative use of a range of audiences, modalities and problem-solving strategies, they become immersed in linguistic, visual, action and spatial knowledge construction. Storytelling about and mapping of community issues supports unfolding of narrative sequences with group input, use of gesture and sometimes drawing. In the performance modules, participants develop rhetorical sequences of argumentation, and persuasive gesture, intonation and movement to enact the role of community leaders. In addition, and equally as important, our work involves supporting pre-service teachers in learning how to design and implement CS SFL approaches in their own future and current classrooms. A mirror within a mirror, our approach with youth is also an approach we develop with our pre-service teachers to support their embodied SFL pedagogical framework.

Praxis

1. Based on your reading of Chapters 1 and 2, how might you think about designing a youth program focused on issues of interest and that are relevant to the youth members? What would you include and why? How would you organize the curriculum?
2. Think about teacher education courses you have experienced or taught. How would your understandings of the readings and activities have benefited or not from working directly with youth at the same time?
3. What do you see as limitations in using our CS SFL praxis with the youth or adult learners you work with? Explain how you would use just those elements that suit the context of your study or work. Try and connect with what Edgar says about his expectations and disappointments with school and community resources for multilingual learners (see the whole transcript of his talk in Appendix A).

Notes

1 We use the term multilingual in this book to include all dialectal and linguistic resources that our participants brought to our collaborative space.
2 See Appendix A for complete transcript of Edgar's talk.
3 Backward design is used to support educators in their curriculum design in thinking about what essential and enduring understandings they want learners to appropriate by the end of the module or year (Wiggins & Tighe, 1998).

References

Abu El-Haj, T. R., & Rubín, B. C. (2009). Realizing the equity-minded aspirations of detracking and inclusion: Toward a capacity-oriented framework for teacher education. *Curriculum Inquiry, 39*(3), 435–463.

Bezemer, J. J., & Kress, G. R. (2016). *Multimodality, learning and communication: A social semiotic frame.* London, UK: Routledge.

Bode, P. (2019). My teaching philosophy. Retrieved May 22, 2019, from http://www.pattybode. com/teaching-philosophy.html

Burke, K. J., Greene, S., & McKenna, M. K. (2016). A critical geographic approach to youth civic engagement: Reframing educational opportunity zones and the use of public spaces. *Urban Education, 51*(2), 143–169. doi:10.1177/0042085914543670.

Burke, K., Harman, R., Hadley, H., & Mizell, J. (2018). I almost feel like I didn't get the chance to really begin': Challenges and opportunities in a critical, project-based clinical experience. *New Educator, 14*(3), 212–230 . doi: 10.1080/1547688X.2017.1407851.

Buxton, C., Harman, R., Cardozo-Gaibisso, L., Lei, J., Bui, K., & Allexsaht-Snider, M. (2019). Understanding science and language connections: New approaches to assessment with bilingual learners. *Research in Science Education, 49*(4), 977–988. doi.org/10.1007/s11165-019-9846-8

Christie, F. (2007). Ongoing dialogue: Functional linguistic and Bernsteinian sociological perspectives on education. In F. Christie & J. R. Martin (Eds.) *Language, knowledge and pedagogy: Functional linguistic and sociological perspectives* (pp. 3–13). London, UK: Continuum.

Cimasko, T., & Shin, D. (2017). Multimodal resemiotization and authorial agency in an L2 writing classroom. *Written Communication, 34*(4), 387–413.

Cochran-Smith, M. (2001). The outcomes question in teacher education. *Teaching & Teacher Education, 17*(5), 527–546. doi:10.1016/S0742-051X(01)00012-9.

García, O. (2009). *Multilingual education in the 21st century: A global perspective.* Oxford, UK: Blackwell.

Gebhard, M. (2019). *Teaching and researching ELLs' disciplinary literacies: Systemic functional linguistics in action in the context of U.S. school reform.* New York, NY: Routledge.

González, N., Moll, L. C., & Amanti, C. (Eds.). (2005). *Funds of knowledge: Theorizing practices in households, communities, and classrooms.* New York, NY: Routledge.

Green, K. (2016). Black 'youth speak truth' to power: Literacy for freedom, community radio, and civic engagement. In S. Green, K. J. Burke, & M. K. McKenna (Eds.) *Youth voices, public spaces, and civic engagement* (pp. 189–209). New York, NY: Routledge.

Greene, S., Burke, K. J., & McKenna, M. (2015). Forms of voice: Exploring the empowerment of youth at the intersection of art and action. *Urban Review, 92*(6), 389–402.

Halliday, M., & Hasan, R. (1989). *Language, context, and text: Aspects of language in a social semiotician perspective* (2nd ed.). Oxford, UK: Oxford University Press.

Halliday, M., & Matthiessen, C. (2004). *An introduction to functional grammar.* London, UK: Arnold.

Halliday, M., McIntosh, A., & Strevens, P. (1964). *The linguistic sciences and language teaching.* Bloomington, IN: Indiana University Press.

Hammond J., & Gibbons, P. (2005). Putting scaffolding to work: The contribution of scaffolding in articulating ESL education. *Prospect Special Issue, 20*(1), 6–30.

Harman, R., Siffrinn, N., Mizell, J., & Bui, K. (in press). Promoting reflection literacy in pre-service language teacher education: Critical SFL praxis with multilingual youth. In L. Altariste & C. Crosby (Eds.), *Second language writing across PK16 contexts: Intersections of teaching, learning, and development.* Ann Arbor, MI: University of Michigan Press.

Harman, R. (Ed.). (2018). *Bilingual learners and social equity: Critical take(s) on systemic functional linguistics.* London, UK: Springer.

Harman, R., Johnson, L., & Chagoya, E. (2016). Bilingual youth voices in middle school: Performance, storytelling and photography. In S. Greene, K. J. Burke, & M. K. McKenna (Eds.) *Youth voices, literacies, and civic engagement* (pp. 210–234). New York, NY: Routledge.

Harman, R., & Khote, N. (2018). Critical SFL Praxis *with* immigrant youth: Multilingual meaning making practices. *Critical Inquiry in Language Studies, 15*(1), 63–83. doi.org/ 10.1080/15427587.2017.1318663

Harman, R., & Shin, D. (2018). Multimodal and community-based literacies: Agentive multilingual learners in elementary school. In G. Onchwari, & J. Keengwe (Eds.) *Handbook of research on pedagogies and cultural considerations for young English language learners* (pp. 217–238). Hershey, PA: IGI Global.

Hasan, R. (1996). Literacy, everyday talk and society. In R. Hasan, & G. Williams (Eds.) *Literacy in society* (pp. 377–424). Harlow, UK: Addison Wesley Longman.

Hasan, R. (2011). *Language and education: Learning and teaching in society.* London, UK: Equinox.

Herbel-Eisenmann, B., Drake, C., & Cirillo, M. (2009). 'Muddying the clear waters': Teacher's take-up of the linguistic idea of revoicing. *Teaching and Teacher Education, 25*(2), 268–277.

Humphrey, S. (2010). Modelling social affiliation and genre in the civic domain. In A. Mahboob, & N. K. Knight (Eds.) *Appliable Linguistics* (pp. 76–91). London, UK: Continuum.

Kinloch, V. (2010). *Harlem on our minds: Place, race, and the literacies of urban youth*. New York, NY: Teachers College Press.

Kress, G. R. (2003). *Literacy in the new media age*. London, UK: Routledge.

Lee, O., Quinn, H., & Valdés, G. (2013). Science and language for English language learners in relation to next generation science standards and with implications for common core state standards for English language arts and mathematics. *Educational Researcher, 42*(4), 223–233. doi: 10.3102/0013189X13480524.

Matthiessen, C. (2018). The notional of a multilingual meaning potential: A systematic exploration. In A. Baklouti, & L. Fontaine (Eds.) *Perspectives on systemic functional linguistics* (pp. 90–120). New York, NY: Routledge.

New London Group. (1996). A pedagogy of multiliteracies: Designing social features. *Harvard Educational Review, 66*(1), 60–92.

Paris, D. (2012). Culturally sustaining pedagogy: A needed change in stance, terminology, and practice. *Educational Researcher, 41*(3), 93–97.

Paris, D., & Alim, H.S. (2017). *Culturally sustaining pedagogies: Teaching and learning for justice in a changing world*. New York, NY: Teachers College Press.

Potts, D. (2018). Critical praxis, design and reflection literacy: A lesson in multimodality. In R. Harman (Ed.) *Bilingual learners and social equity: Critical approaches to systemic functional linguistics* (pp. 201–224). Cham, Switzerland: Springer International.

Rubin, B. C., Abu El-Haj, T. R., Graham, E., & Clay, K. (2016). Confronting the urban civic opportunity gap: Integrating youth participatory action research into teacher education. *Journal of Teacher Education, 67*(5), 424–436.

Schleppegrell, M. (2013). The role of meta-language in supporting academic language development. *Language Learning, 63*(1), 153–170.

Schleppegrell, M., & Moore, J. (2018). Linguistic tools for supporting emergent critical language awareness in the elementary school. In R. Harman (Ed.) *Bilingual learners and social equity: Critical approaches to systemic functional linguistics* (pp. 23–43). New York, NY: Springer.

Semali, L. M. (2002). *Transmediation in the classroom: A semiotics-based media literacy framework*. New York, NY: Peter Lang.

Sharma, A., & Buxton, C. (2018). *The natural world and science education in the United States*. London, UK: Palgrave.

Siffrinn, N., & Harman, R. (2019). Toward an embodied systemic functional linguistics. *TESOL Quarterly, 53*(4), 909–1193.

Simon, H. A. (1996). *The sciences of the artificial*. Cambridge, MA: MIT Press.

Tuck, E., & Yang, K. W. (2014). R-words: Refusing research. In D. Paris & M. Winn (Eds.) *Humanizing research: Decolonizing qualitative inquiry with youth and communities* (pp. 223–247). Thousand Oaks, CA: SAGE.

Vygotsky, L. S. (1978). *Mind in society: the development of higher psychological processes*. Cambridge, MA: Harvard University Press.

Williams, G. (2000). Children's literature, children and uses of language description. In L. Unsworth (Ed.) *Researching language in schools and communities: Functional linguistic perspectives* (pp. 111–129). London, UK: Cassell.

Wiggins, G., & McTighe, J. (1998). *Understanding by design*. Alexandria, VA: ASCD.

Winn, L. T., & Winn, M. T. (2016). 'We want this to be owned by you': The promise and perils of youth participatory action research. In S. Greene, K. J. Burke, & M. K. McKenna (Eds.) *Youth voices, literacies, and civic engagement* (pp. 111–130). New York, NY: Routledge.

Yancy, G. (2008). *Black bodies, white gazes: The continuing significance of race.* Lanham, MD: Rowman & Littlefield.

Appendix A: My thoughts: Edgar Chagoya

"The art work just kept building me up": My involvement in CS SFL Programs

Ladies and Gentlemen, I want to ruminate about a struggle that today's youth has to deal with or has dealt with for generations. Communication. Confidence. And I think that the CS SFL praxis and programs like that support students, the youth, to build up that confidence to build a pathway into good connections, to actually succeed in life, to get to represent what they believe in, to represent their societies, to represent what they've seen.

In 2013 I came here, but before that I always felt supported by my family and my community back in Mexico. I always felt confident and it felt like I had good communication skills, and after my family decided to come to the United States I had a big struggle with that. I lost confidence, I lost my communication, especially my communication, as I had no English vocabulary, probably I just knew the colors, the numbers and some animals. I clearly didn't take any English classes in any way before. I was going blindly into a new environment, in which I had to adapt. And that was really hard for me, as I just struggled. In my struggle I noticed that I and many other students out there, who have a great potential, are not able to achieve their goals yet because they have not been given the resources necessary to actually step up. The youth, including myself, we need help to actually step up.

But nowadays we are expected to follow the standards, the strict testing, which really just takes a lot of our time and we really try to focus on school and other materials that yes we will use them eventually in time, but sometimes really we need to focus on real communication, on building confidence. Schools really don't focus on that; I haven't seen a class in my school which strictly supports this. Because these are skills we all know we're going to use eventually in life. These skills are necessary to actually go through and build all the legacy before you. After I came here, I found myself in a situation with other multilingual people in a program called ESOL, which is English as Second Language for students. And I met other people in the same situation, and I knew it wasn't just me. I wasn't alone in this struggle, this journey, of trying to get my point across. It was really hard to deal with, and after some time they introduced me to Ruth. I'm really glad I met her, and other people I have met through the CS SFL praxis because they helped me build up my confidence back again, to recreate my earlier communication ways in Mexico. Also, through the artistic projects and storytelling, they helped me stand up for those people that keep on struggling right now in my school, students I have been with for years but who just couldn't get through it. And they help me to build myself.

After I began working in the arts program with Ruth and others in fall 2013, I created my story about coming to the United States and the passage to school here. It was really hard in the arts program as at that time I did not speak English yet; I had to use a friend/translator as well to help me out when we shared our stories with the general public of Athens who can't speak Spanish. We also used photography and that semiotic process helped me to understand meaning behind the symbols we used.

The art work just kept on helping me and building me up, all of that confidence. Those projects just pushed me into understanding how I would have to carve that space for now to help others get there as well. And after I joined the CS SFL program as a leader three years later, I knew I already knew English, but I just couldn't help going back to help the people, who were in the same situation that I was and seeing the situation had not changed at all, as when I was in that situation. There were students just like me who had come, and were really in need of help, and it was the same situation. And when I came in, I just kind of saw the reflection of myself. And the cycle, the paradox continuing on just being there and nobody being able to do anything about it. Us not having the power to influence that as we keep on making the gap between people who need more help but also in the CS SFL workshops we try to advance more, we try to actually help the students who need a lot of help, we actually spend more time on that.

I feel like art brings a creative side of a person, and that's something I value, because it allows me to reflect on everything I see and that's something I love to do. As I reflect on society I reflect on what's happening, the government, you reflect on all that things you see, all the things the media are giving you to see, the bad moments, it brings you out and lets you see things from a bigger perspective. And even though you see so many bad things you want to change what you cannot change, looking inside of you to find a way to express yourself, it just kind of brings it out there and you're doing something not just for anybody else, but yourself to express what you feel about what's happening in our societies and it just kind of expresses what you feel and if other people understand the same thing as you, you will feel great as you are sending a message even if it's through art or through something that's hidden, it's just really advancing into that and bringing it out there without speaking.

And helping out with the multilinguals, people from this last program in CS SFL 2017 we were working in, it was great. I was able to help them, and I was able to see how this struggle that they had was actually getting worse and worse.

Because the standardized testing brought them more down, their confidence, because they couldn't do anything about, they still had to take the same test, they had some accommodation which did not help as much as it should. They just had to take the same test, seeing the same results, which just led them to more disappointment in themselves, because they cannot focus on both things, learning the language and understanding building up into that side, or actually advancing on learning about the material that we're expected to learn. Even people who know perfect English struggle with the material that we have to, or actually teachers have to go through. It's just extensive they have to go through all this material, break it down even further which still doesn't help because they still rush everything into it, and I don't see that helping as much, because we can see that most of the time we're not learning, we're memorizing content for the test, and keep on advancing into that placement. We just memorize, take the test and then forget everything we learn.

And I really think supporting this kind of CS SFL program breaks through that. Helps us build up that confidence, helps us look for those resources to change that cycle that keeps on getting us nowhere.

PRELUDE TO CHAPTER 3

Relationship Building and Critical Community Engagement

In Chapters 1 and 2 we introduced you to the *CS SFL* praxis we have designed and implemented in youth programs in the southeast part of the United States. Chapter 3, written by Jason Mizell, centers the insights and lived experiences of participants of color in our programs, who are at full center of the work (Nieto & Bode, 2018 ; Paris & Alim, 2017). Indeed, this chapter is a pivotal part of our book because it highlights the deep, caring and long-lasting relationships that provoked critical conversations and research among adult and youth members in our institute (Mulligan & Nadarajah, 2008). Specifically, in this chapter Jason Mizell, a Black bilingual community activist and university researcher, provides a deep account of how he came to this work. He also discusses how he and his co-researchers in our youth programs used Latine Critical Race (LatCrit) methodologies to engage in collaborative inquiry about their lives in a highly conservative southern state.

As clearly demonstrated in Jason's relationship with his co-researchers, emotions of trust, joy, anger and frustration were central to the experience of the group as they assumed multiple literate and civic identities in their work together (Leander & Frank, 2006). This relational aspect of community engagement is vital to our CS SFL praxis in that it disrupts normative power dynamics and supports counter storytelling through involvement of both intellectual and affective domains (Harman, Johnson, & Chagoya, 2016). Without such establishment of caring and longitudinal relationships among our participants, our work has little or no meaning. As Kinloch (2016) stated:

> A paradigmatic shift is needed, one that is no longer grounded in individualism, competition, and inequality but in collaboration (e.g., ongoing exchange of ideas and collaboration as respectful and reciprocal),

empathy (e.g., that results from critical listening and a discourse of care), and humanization. (p. 91)

When reading the following chapter, we encourage readers—whether teachers, community activists, students or researchers—to think about how you can relate in affective and intellectual ways with your youth co-researchers and students. How can you establish open relationships that are trusting, critical and longitudinal?

References

Harman, R., Johnson, L., & Chagoya, E. (2016). Bilingual youth voices in middle school: Performance, storytelling and photography. In S. Greene, K. J. Burke, & M. K. McKenna (Eds.) *Youth voices, literacies, and civic engagement* (pp. 210–234). New York, NY: Routledge.

Kinloch, V. (2016). Publicly engaged scholarship in urban communities: Possibilities for literacy teaching and learning. In S. Greene, K. Burke, & M. K. McKenna (Eds.) *Youth voices, public spaces, and civic engagement* (pp. 88–110). New York, NY: Routledge.

Leander, K. M., & Frank, A. (2006). The aesthetic production and distribution of image/subjects among online youth. *E-Learning, 3*(2), 185–206.

Mulligan, M., & Nadarajah, Y. (2008). Working on the sustainability of local communities with a 'community-engaged' research methodology. *Local Environment, 13*(2), 81–94.

Nieto, S., & Bode, P. (2018). *Affirming diversity: The sociopolitical context of multicultural education* (7th ed.). Boston, MA: Pearson/Allyn and Bacon.

Paris, D., & Alim, H. S. (2017). *Culturally sustaining pedagogies: Teaching and learning for justice in a changing world*. New York, NY: Teachers College Press.

3

TESTIMONIOS: DEVELOPING RELATIONSHIPS TO NURTURE CIVIC ENGAGEMENT AND LEARNING

Jason Mizell

Jason's Testimonio

As Hurston wrote, "there is no greater agony than bearing an untold story inside you" (1942, p. 121). My story began decades ago in a small rural town in Northeastern Georgia. It was in my hometown that I learned that untold stories or testimonios from my community were important as a way of centering the truths of minoritized communities. As a young Black boy who attended majority white[1] elementary, middle and high schools, I learned early on that the "stories" or counternarratives that my mom and others told me were more than just casual stories. I learned that they held meaning and lessons. Lessons that would help me survive in a world that wasn't built for me.

I remember coming home from elementary school one day and telling my mother that I had been put in one of the lowest reading groups and that everyone in that group was Black. My mother listened attentively and then told me how it was when she was in elementary school in another small southern town a few hours southeast of where we lived. She told me that before the end of segregation, the Black teachers in her school pushed her and her friends to be successful. The expectation and belief held by her Black teachers was that every Black child could and would be successful. My mother went on to tell me that her teachers had wanted her to skip from first grade to third grade because she was so smart and capable. She also stated that after her school was integrated and most of the Black teachers were replaced with white teachers, she was placed in a remedial reading group. She went from being acknowledged as reading two years above grade level to supposedly reading below grade level in less than one year. The only way that she was able to get out of that group she told me was by working five times as hard as the white kids. She looked me in the eye and said, "Jason you are Black and if you want to succeed, you have to work twice as hard to get half as far."

My experiences throughout elementary, middle, high school and college were true to my mom's counter story. My mom's counternarrative was/is a mirror, window and sliding glass door (Bishop, 1990) in that it allowed me to see a reflection of myself in her story (mirror); it allowed me to catch a glimpse of her life (window); and it has provided a way for me to truly come to empathize with her by "stepping" into her life (sliding glass door) to learn from her and also to understand that I wasn't and am not alone. As a queer trilingual (African-American English (AAE)-dominant American English (DAE)-Spanish) Black man, born in the American South but having lived over half of my life in South America, the testimonios of my communities (in the United States and the Global South) and in particular those of my family have driven me to become passionate about our *Culturally Sustaining Systemic Functional Linguistics (CS SFL)* work.

Sharing my untold stories with my co-researchers (youth and adult) in our summer and after school programs allowed them to see and understand me (Paris, 2011; Paris & Winn, 2013). Opening myself up to them and freely owning my various identities through rich and profound dialogic conversations fell in line with Paris's (2011) work on humanizing research when he stated that youth participants:

> Demanded that I claim identities and experiences in the ways I was continually asking them to do in the somewhat dialogic process we call ethnography....This genuine and honest sharing led to richer and truer data than the model of the somewhat detached, neutral researcher that echoes across the decades from more positivist-influenced versions of qualitative inquiry. (p. 139)

The demand for sharing wasn't just from the youth but also from the adult co-researchers. We all wanted and needed to know the stories or testimonios of those with whom we were working. Knowing what brought them to our critically oriented work helped us to build community and a shared purpose.

A vital part of our CS SFL work is relationship building. Sharing our testimonios functioned as a way to destabilize and deconstruct the white gaze (Yancy, 2008). We could focus not just on our pain but also on our joys. The joys that have allowed minoritized communities to survive and dream of a "*literacy of* pleasure and joy" (Wong & Peña, 2017, p. 118). Through the white gaze, knowledge is valued only if it conforms to a Eurocentric measuring stick. For instance, David Stoll (2008, p. xxv), widely known for his attempt to discredit Rigoberto Menchú (2018), expressed that one of his main reasons for not wanting to accept her testimonio was that it established "a new standard of truth gaining ground in the humanities and social sciences." Testimonios provide a platform for voices of the subaltern (Orelus, 2018) (i.e., those who have been minoritized and framed as less than by those in power [Gramsci, 2005]) to be heard and valued as legitimate knowledge (Kubota, 2019; Pérez-Huber, 2012). Our CS SFL work centers the joys, truths, questionings, knowledges and literacy practices of our communities.

The following sections provide a description of Critical Race Theory (CRT) and Latine[2] Critical Race Theory (LatCrit). I explain why this lens supported youth and adults in our programs to convey their testimonios and counternarratives; and how it also helped me and can help others who wish to be accomplices of youth as they strive to become critical consumers and producers of knowledge. It will also challenge you, the reader, to think about how you can actively listen to, respond to, and center the testimonios of youth in your own work.

CS SFL Praxis and LatCrit

This chapter was conceptualized through a LatCrit framework, which grew out of CRT. CRT is a powerful theoretical lens that enables researchers and practitioners to explore how race and power dynamics are interconnected within dominant ideologies, laws and policies (Harper, Patton, & Wooden, 2009; Taylor, Gillborn, & Ladson-Billings, 2016). The approach centers the knowledge(s) of racially minoritized communities and decenters Eurocentric meritocracy and supremacy (Bernal & Villalpando, 2002; Crenshaw, Gotanda, Peller, & Thomas, 1995; Delgado & Stefancic, 2000). In our programs, a CRT critique of K-12 institutions helps us to see and challenge racialized policies and practices.

LatCrit developed out of CRT as a way to attend to the interplay of languaging[3] practices (i.e., bilingualism/multilingualism), immigration/migration and ethnicity in the lives of Latine communities (Bernal, 2002). It disrupts the Black-white binary of racial relationships generally adopted in the United States in establishing race remedy laws and/or procedures (Stefancic, 1997). LatCrit provides a nuanced view of racism through its historical view of language practices (bilingualism or multilingualism), immigration status, experiential knowledge, in addition to "other forms of subordination (e.g., class, gender, language)" (Rodriguez, 2011, p. 241. One way that LatCrit attends to experiential knowledge is by utilizing testimonios as a method and methodology that allows minoritized communities and individuals to bear witness to their truths (Pérez-Huber, 2012).

Testimonios: More Than Just Stories

Testimonios are lived histories/personal accounts or stories that Latines recount to let others learn about their lived truths, either as individuals or to represent communal lived experiences. Oral traditions—such as *dichos, adivinazas, consejos and cuentos [or testimonios]*—have played an important role in the lives of indigenous communities in the Americas since the times of the Maya (Fien, n.d. Menchú-Tum & Gugelberger, 1998; Smith, Flores, & González, 2015). Similarly, in Black culture counternarratives have been used since slavery and reportedly even before in much the same way (Baszile, 2015). Not only do testimonios and counternarratives act as affirming text, they also act as revolutionary text that can help to refocus dominant narratives. As powerful text, they can be shared as oral histories, photographs, (Del Vecchio, Toomey, & Tuck, 2017), written text or through other modes (Eggins, 2004) such as 3D models or dramas (e.g., legislative theater). As potentially powerful multimodal representations and witness to the lived experiences of people of color, testimonios are an integral part of CS SFL praxis. They provide numerous ways for minoritized communities to have their voices heard and acted upon.

Testimonios also morph the traditional roles of researcher and researched to co-researchers, where the researcher and participant become co-constructors of knowledge through a process of collaborative data production, collection, dialog and analysis. This aspect of testimonios played itself out throughout every aspect of our CS SFL work. The youth with whom we worked and their *vecinos* and *parientes* were central in helping us to construct, validate and remix knowledges as we jointly worked together. This process of co-construction of knowledge helped to decenter hegemonic ways of understanding how educational research "should" be carried out (Huber, 2012).

As powerful generative text, testimonios helped my co-researchers and me to locate ourselves and our communities in dialogic conversations as we examined our context through various historical, linguistic, social and cultural lenses. They have the power to support minoritized students and others in finding mirrors, windows and sliding glass doors (Bishop, 1990). In this chapter I use the terms testimonios and counternarratives interchangeably, although I understand they have slightly different origins.

Centering Ourselves in the Telling

This section introduces three of the more than 30 youth with whom I studied and co-researched between 2016 and 2018. These focal youth were chosen in large part because of their desire to have their stories shared widely and because their testimonios echo those of the other youth in our CS SFL projects.

Cierra[4]

I first met Cierra during the summer of 2016 when we were randomly paired together during the first CS SFL program, which was part of Camp SPLASH. Camp SPLASH was a month-long K-8 summer camp jointly coordinated by the Parkside County School District and a large land grant state university located in the American Southeast. 2016 was the first year of the camp and the CS SFL course, described in Chapter 1 in greater detail. At that time, Cierra was a 14-year-old rising eighth grader who lived near the site of the summer camp in a large public housing community. As Cierra and I got to know each other, we found that we shared many things in common. We are both Black, labeled as having a learning disability and living or having lived in a public housing, single parent mother-led household. Although we had those things in common, there were also differences based on gender, age, and of course, life experiences. However, because of the deep and trusting bond that we developed during Camp SPLASH, Cierra advocated for our work to continue in the empty community center in her public housing complex. Thanks to her vision, we developed an agreement with the housing authority and university in our town and successfully opened the center for literacy and art programs. We also obtained funding so that Cierra and her mother could attend a national applied linguistics conference where we presented our joint work. Our collaboration has also allowed me to deepen ties with her family, especially with her mother and younger sister. We often talk about community issues, school concerns and life in general. Her mother has also become an unofficial advocate for the community center programs.

Simón

Simón and I first met during Spring 2017 when I co-taught a master's level English as a Second Language (ESOL) content-based course at his middle school. The course was the first school-based iteration of the CS SFL Institute (see description of the programs in Chapter 1). At the time of our meeting, Simón was 14 and had only been in the United States for a couple of years. He had immigrated from Central America in order to escape death threats at the hands of various gangs that had taken over his community. As a result of his relatively recent arrival into the local school district, he had been labeled as an Emergent Bilingual Learner (EBL). Simón and I found that we had a great deal in common due to our experiences of living in Latin America. Although we had lived in different Latin American countries and were from different generations, we found that we got along very well due to a shared language, valuing of community connections and love of similar musical genres, especially an appreciation for hip hop and reggaeton. After Simón graduated from the middle school and was in ninth grade at the feeder high school, he reached out to me and asked if he could participate in the second year of the CS SFL program in Spring 2018. Simón and Lucia, another youth co-researcher, and I also spent hours at a sound studio, located on the campus of the local university, recording their rap songs. Because the building of close communal ties is a vital part of the culturally sustaining nature of the CS SFL work, we have also spent time together breaking bread with his family and with other community members on various occasions.

Edgar

Edgar was a brilliant and dynamic 15-year-old Mexican national when we first met in Spring 2016. He had previously been involved in several different youth-related projects carried out by Ruth Harman. When he began collaborating with Ruth, Edgar took part in a community-based writing project and as a result was a co-author on several published articles and book chapters based on his testimonios. At the time of our meeting, he expressed his desire to help other bilingual youth so that they would not feel alone as they worked to understand their new lives in the United States. He came into our school-based CS SFL project in 2017 as a peer-mentor and as an experienced co-researcher and learner. At that time, he was the only high school student in our group. Since 2016, Edgar and I have had the opportunity to co-lead and present at two national conferences and to present a two-day workshop to a combined university and community audience in New England. Outside of the project, Edgar and I often speak about our dreams for the future and how we hope that we can support our communities. Recently, we mapped out a tour of college campuses that he and my son would like to visit.

The testimonios of Cierra, Simon and Edgar are distinct but also representative of the lives of many of our youth co-participants. They most often found our co-constructed CS SFL programs powerful and meaningful. They felt that the focus on community problem-solving and multimodality showed a respect of their cultures and knowledge(s); they also felt that the programs helped them to develop intergenerational relationships with diverse adults from the community and university.

Testimonios and Counternarratives

The testimonios that are retold here are presented with as much fidelity as possible to their original meanings. They are drawn from the numerous conversations (i.e., oral conversations, Facebook messenger conversations and text messages) that my co-researchers and I had over the last several years. Due to the necessity to modify them somewhat from their original mode (oral conversations held either in African-American English (AAE) and/or Spanish, textspeak and models) to a written academic format, some changes were necessary. Due to the fact that I had to weave together and move through and across different modes and heteroglossic contexts (Khote & Tian, 2019), I freely offer up that in this retelling of my co-participants testimonios, I am the filter. I act as an interpreter or interlocutor of meaning as I work to process the original statements of my co-knowledge generators as I select the words and grammatical structures that I present below (Esposito, 2001). Latine scholar Judith Flores Carmona (2014) stated that in the process of translating as the "researcher/participant, we straddled together between lenguas and cross cultures, entre mundos" (p. 119). Translating or weaving together the languaging of someone else was/is more than just repeating words from one language or mode to another; it is working to honestly express culturally specific nuances that are expressed not just orally or bodily but, in many cases, multimodally.

As the interlocutor, I take my job as remixer of languages, cultures and modes seriously as I work to translate their stories from one or multiple languages, contexts and modes to another so that their voices, thoughts and intentions can be shared. With this in mind, as co-constructors of knowledge, my co-researchers and I jointly worked to "bring [their] situation[s] to the attention of an audience—the public sphere—to which [they] would normally not have access because of the very conditions of subalternity to which [their] testimonio bears witness" (Beverly, 2000, p. 572). One central aspect of CS SFL is its focus on making sure that the languages, cultures and knowledges of the subaltern are valued inherently and thus afforded a central place in the "public sphere."

The testimonios that follow allow a glimpse into how my youth co-researchers processed their feelings (i.e., love, joy, pain, anger and hope) about their communities, schools and also their knowledge of racism and exclusion. These counterstories allow us to glimpse how one Black female teenager and two Latine teenagers from different countries of origin viewed and experienced their world(s). Their stories also help us to hear from them on how important they felt it was to build strong communal relationships intergenerationally and how those relationships helped them to become active critical consumers and producers of literacy as they became civic agents in their communities.

The following testimonios are composite stories (Cook & Dixson, 2013; Tafari, 2018) in that they are drawn from our numerous dialogic conversations that took place over the last three years. They will be presented with minimal interpretation so that the testimonista's voice can be heard.

Cierra

The following composite conversation took place during the summer of 2016. Cierra, I and several other co-researchers (youth and adults) discussed the book *Tar Beach* (Ringgold, 1991) and how we felt about our schools. In what follows, Cierra's testimonio that I have translated from oral AAE is based on her feelings about the book, her school and her relationships with the other participants of the CS SFL program. The excerpt highlights what she likes and dislikes about some of the work we did together in the program, crucial feedback for us in doing this work. She also shared what brought her joy:

> We read a book and it talked about racism. [We read the book Tar Beach[5] (Ringgold, 1991)]....It was mostly about the projects, and about racism. It was a good book. It relates to people that lives in apartments and projects. A very long time [ago]. And um, it was good. It was a good book. And you had enjoyed it too. And Monday, Monday was good. I had fun. What I like about it was how we [they] had a good advice, for people, advice about kids. And what I then like was the book talking about racism. I know that happened back in the day, but you still don't have to bring it up.
>
> It is just fun hanging out with y'all guys and getting to talk to y'all guys and giving y'all guys advice when y'all become a teacher and things. And my day was good, yeah.
>
> I didn't really think of racism like it was in the book, in that way. I just felt; I don't know. I mean, some teachers they act mean towards to you, to me, because of my color, but I don't know. It probably just me thinking like that.
>
> Sometimes if like I asked a teacher what the answer to something is like they are mean to me but help the white kids and they go like eh, you can go find the answer. Or something like that.
>
> It bothers me to talk about it. Because I feel like they was treated, I mean, not trying to say this in any race, but I feel like back then white people treated black people wrong so many times, in so many ways. I mean, everybody could have been treated equally and how people want to be treated, but it seems like they wanted to treat us like trash, ...I don't like talking about it because I just feel bad about it.
>
> I want to help you guys when you become teachers to know about kids. I like to give advice so that for people, advice about kids. So, you can more help with kids who struggle in their classes.
>
> More teachers in the class, and teachers who support, more support classes. And like, if you don't, if you didn't pass all your classes, they should help you get into summer school and all that. Most teachers are ready to see us fail.
>
> And it is just, it's just fun hanging out with y' all guys and getting to talk to y'all and giving y'all advice if when y'all become a teacher or anything and ummm....and ummm, my day was good and yeah
>
> I like talking to Jason, he listens. Here y'all listen so if I have a bad day you listen to me. When I need—when I'm having trouble with something or don't understand, he'll help me out no matter what it is.
>
> We need teachers who can help us no matter!

Cierra continued by sharing her insights about her public housing complex:

Parkside Public Housing community needs to be rebuilt. They be mold everywhere. We have [a community] center. It was closed down after they held a funeral there. Ever since, now we don't have nowhere to go. That's what we should do [Help the community]. Like, go and pick up trash and or help, like, buying food and give to the homeless. We could also uh-huh, …get to help the community. Parkside is a place that people live. It is a place for people who need a place to live. It don't matter who they are. Parkside is a place for people who need a home.

Simón

During the first couple of weeks of working with students at Parkside Middle School, participants were asked to share as much or as little as they desired about their lives in small multi-age-race-and linguistic groups. Simón honored and trusted the group by willingly sharing part of his immigration story. This is his story that I have translated from Spanish.

When I was 12 years old, I left my home country with my sister. We had to leave because gangs were killing people. They were trying to get me to join them just like they had with my older brother and dad. My mom and dad had left years before because of the same thing. The gangs threatened to kill my dad if he didn't join. My mom told me and you (Jason) that when my older brother was a baby that some gang members took him from her and said that if my dad didn't join the gang that they would kidnap and kill him. I remember walking to school from my grandparents' house and seeing dead bodies. There was this one guy whose head was smashed in, I guess he didn't want to be in the gang or [that the gang] did something to him. I don't know. I was scared all the time. I didn't want to join but they were always trying to get me to join. They said they were going to hurt me and my sister. My grandparents knew it was dangerous, but we had to leave. My sister and I started walking and everything for a long time. One day she fell and twisted her ankle and I had to help carry her. My mother didn't want us to be separated but when we finally arrived at the border somewhere in Texas, they took my sister and left me. I went to this farmer's house, but he wasn't home. His son was mean. He locked me and this other guy in a grain bin. We were in there I guess for about a week with hardly any food or water. When the farmer came back, I don't know where he was…he was mad at his son. He said that we could sleep in his house and take a shower in his bathroom. A few days later, this truck came to take me away. We were on the road, like a highway and the migra came and stopped the truck. They took me to the refrigerator[6]. It was you know, a place that they take kids who aren't with their parents. I was there for about two weeks. It was so cold there. I was finally able to call my mom. She was here in Georgia. She was crying and stuff. I had to go to court and talk to a judge. I had to go alone. I was just twelve. They had me sign papers. I don't even remember what I signed. I was a little kid. He told me that I could go see my mom but that I would have to go to court again. They put me on a plane, and I got to Atlanta and my mom was there waiting for me. The trip from my country was scary but I had to do it. The gang was going to kill me.

Now that I am here it is hard. I have to make sure that I do everything perfectly so that I don't get in trouble. I can't be a kid and do stuff like everyone else. I have to be perfect. I have to work and help out, I just don't know what is going to happen now. Trump even got rid of TPS. Now my family is always scared. We can't go back. They sent my uncle back and the gang killed him. They even killed one of my aunts.

You know that I like working with you. I get a chance to learn about things from a different perspective. Plus, I know that you and Ruth try to help me. You are always supporting me. That is why I keep coming back. I don't forget the people that help me. We have to help each other. That way we can learn a lot of stuff together.

Edgar

The following conversation in part took place while Edgar and I were preparing a presentation to present our work to a community action group in the northeast of the United States.

When I first arrived here in the United States, I didn't really know any English. It was hard for me. When I was in Mexico, I knew everyone, and I could go wherever I wanted. I came here and I couldn't go anywhere. I didn't understand anyone. I didn't know anyone other than my cousin. At first, school was so hard. The good thing was that there were a couple of teachers that were good to me. They were my ESOL teachers. They really worked to help me. I met Ruth and other people when I did Rabbit Box. It is this writing and performance group. We wrote about our stories, where we were from and stuff like that. The first time that I had to perform or discuss my story, I had to read it in Spanish and a friend translated it for me in English. The next time that I presented my story, I was able to do it in English. Since I started working with Ruth and the project, I have been able to write a couple of book chapters and articles with her and other people. They take my ideas and opinions seriously. They listen to me. Every time that I can, I keep on working with the group because I feel that I need to give back. I have even learned a little about Systemic Functional Linguistics and how language works. It makes a difference when adults work with you and value what you have to say. They open chances for you to help other people who are sort of in your shoes.

Now that I am almost ready to finish high school things are getting really hard. Here in Georgia, I won't be allowed to study at the top universities because of my immigration status. Plus, they want to charge me as if I don't live here. If I go to a university here, I'll have to pay what foreigners pay. I'm not a foreigner, I've been here since middle school. I live here, my family lives here. Georgia is my home. It makes me sad and sometimes depressed to think that next year for my senior year, I may have to move so that I will be able to study at a university without having to pay as if I were a foreigner. I don't want to have to leave my family and friends, but I know that if I want to honor the sacrifice that my parents have made for me, I may have to leave. All of this gets me down sometimes, but I am not going to give up! I'm just grateful that I met everyone and that I am part of this community.

Collaborative Analysis of the Testimonios

Through pláticas (Fierros & Delgado Bernal, 2016; Flores Carmona, Hamzeh, Bejarano, & Hernández Sánchez, 2018; Guajardo & Guajardo, 2013) or detailed dialogic interpersonal conversations with my youth co-participants, we were able to jointly arrive at an understanding of their testimonios. Over the course of the last year, I met with my co-participants numerous times to discuss and build on our work together. During those times, I also shared with them the above version of their testimonios to make sure that I had understood and recorded them faithfully and so that they could make any changes they deemed necessary. This process also allowed our pláticas to grow and that also expanded our joint understanding of their testimonios. Through our dialogic conversations or pláticas, we negotiated our understanding of their testimonios and how through them others might be able to learn from their lived experiences. Out of our pláticas and revisiting the work that we jointly produced during the various CS SFL projects, several different themes emerged. The themes that we identified were:

- Structural racism
- Benefits of building intergenerational relationships
- Desire to help our community(ies)

These themes are explored in more detail in the following subsections.

Denial of Structural Racism

Research has shown that Black students, in particular, along with other minoritized students are disproportionately punished in K-12 settings (Heilbrun, 2018; Wallace, Goodkind, Wallace, & Bachman, 2008; Welsh & Little, 2018). This has led to what many refer to as the school-to-prison-pipeline/nexus or school pushout (Morris, 2016). When socio-economic and other factors are taken into consideration, the one factor that repeatedly appears to influence the frequency and severity of punishments that are delivered in K-12 settings are students' minoritized status (Heilbrun, Cornell, & Konold, 2018). Research has shown that students who are subjected to punitive measures in school—suspension and expulsion among them—are more likely not to graduate from high school; they also tend to have lower grades and limited educational and employment possibilities after their secondary education.

Although Cierra did not want to talk about racism, she was very cognizant of how it impacted her educational experience. In her counterstory, she reflected on how she was treated differently than her white classmates when she asked for help in school. In a follow-up interview, she stated she wished that teachers were willing to help when Black kids asked for it. She even mentioned that when a Black kid insisted that teachers facilitate their learning, they were viewed as being disrespectful and sent to in-school suspension, something that didn't happen to the white kids in her classes. She stated:

> [This one teacher] would try to send you to ISS [in-school suspension] just for sharpening a pencil. And she would just try to get you in trouble for literally the smallest thing. Like, she would only like, let's say the class was talking. She would only try to send the Black people to ISS and she would act like she didn't see the white people talking.

Situations like this disturbed Cierra because she knew that they limited her educational opportunities. In a conversation that I had with Cierra and her mother, her mother discussed her own time in school. She told us that what was happening with Cierra also happened with her. That when she and other Black kids needed help and asked for it, teachers would tell them that they didn't have the time or they would ignore them. This went on for years and played a large role in her dropping out of school. Her non-completion of high school has impacted her current situation and inability to obtain a decent paying job. In response to what her mother told us, Cierra stated that "It's the same now but I want to finish school. I want to be either a pediatrician and work with drug babies or a nurse. I just need them, teachers, to care and help me."

Cierra wasn't the only one of my co-researchers to have lived through events that were racist. During our frequent conversations, Simón often spoke about the conflicts that he lived at school and also within the Parkside county community. As a un(der)documented (Pérez Rhym, 2017) teenager who was deemed by the school system as having limited English proficiency, he found that many teachers did not take the time to let him organize his thoughts so that he could participate in classroom discussions. He stated, "many times they won't even call on me or when I try to answer they don't give me time to explain myself. There are a couple of teachers who won't even let me ask my friends questions in Spanish so that I can understand what is going on in class." Unfortunately, his experiences were not confined to school. Within the larger community, he and his family were also subjected to discriminatory practices. When his brother was in a car accident caused by a drunk driver, his brother wasn't able to press charges. As Simón told me, "we couldn't do anything, if we did the police would come and arrest my brother and us because we don't have papers, that is what the cop told us when we got to the hospital to see my brother. They had him handcuffed to the bed. As soon as he was able to leave the hospital, we just left and never pressed charges because if we did, they could arrest my brother. That's not right, just because he doesn't have papers." This was one of many situations where it was obvious that his lack of immigration papers was used against him and his family.

A few months after this discussion as Simón and I were driving to Parkside Middle School to take part in an afternoon CS SFL project, he expressed his fear of things to come because President Trump had revoked TPS (temporary protected status) (Weiss, 2018) for several Central American countries. "What are we going to do now, I don't know what is going to happen with my parents? Trump just hates anyone who speaks Spanish! Even more than before, I have to make sure that I don't get in trouble. The other day the ex-boyfriend of this girl that I like told me that he is going to call *la migra* if I don't stop talking to her." Intuitively, Simón was able to understand that racist ideologies were behind the problems that impacted his daily life.

Although Edgar's story in many ways is different from Simón's in that his family came to the United States seeking a way to provide a more economically stable life rather than trying to escape gang violence, he also has had to confront structural racism. In 2010, the University System of Georgia Board of Regents issued a decree that effectively denied qualified un(der)documented students from applying to top state institutions of higher learning (University System of Georgia, 2010). It also reinforced the practice of charging un(der)documented students who had been educated in Georgia K-12 schools and who had lived in the state for years out-of-state tuition rates. This declaration established a two-tier system of education in the state of Georgia. Students who were able to prove their U.S. citizenship had the opportunity to continue their post-secondary education at some of the most prestigious universities in the American Southeast. By contrast, academically talented un(der) documented youth were explicitly told that they were unwanted and considered second-class students. It did not matter that in most cases they had been educated for the majority of their lives in Georgia public schools. This is the reality that Edgar is facing. As he looks to the future, he is struggling as he tries to decide what to do. In one text-message exchange, he stated, "pero es muy posible que me mude por la escuela, college el siguiente año. Es triste situacion. Si es triste pero tengo que hacer lo que tengo y aveces me desanima pero no te preocupes no me rendiré tan facilmente/it is very possible that I'll have to move next year for school. The situation is sad. It is sad but I have to do what I have to do. Sometimes I feel like I can't go on, I lose hope but don't worry, I'm not going to give up that easily."

CS SFL as an explicitly anti-racist pedagogy helped me and my co-researchers to openly talk about our experiences with racism and more importantly the institutional linguistic ideologies that reenforce them. Through a valuing of our testimonios and how they helped us to generate knowledge, CS SFL promoted a complicating and extending of what was relevant to our lived experiences.

An interesting and unexpected finding in relation to institutional racism was that two of my co-researchers mentioned episodes in which they were treated differently based on their race, place of origin and/or languaging practices yet they did not want to call those actions racist when explicitly asked if they had ever experienced racism. In Cierra's testimonio, she acknowledged racism while also stating that she didn't want to talk about it. She even seemed to want to push knowledge of it away when she stated, "I didn't really think of racism like it was in the book [Tar Beach], in that way. I just felt I don't know. I mean, some teachers they act mean towards to you, to me, because of my color, *but I don't know. It probably just got me thinking like that*." Simón reacted similarly when during one of our conversations I asked him if teachers treated him differently based on where he was from and his languaging practices. He said, "No gracias a dios nunca/*no thank God*." He made that statement even though in his testimonio and our subsequent conversations, he has mentioned multiple times that some teachers and even classmates react negatively toward him when he speaks Spanish.

Teeger in her 2015 article puts forth the argument of "both sides of the story." Her argument is that the "both sides of the story" argument is cultivated within schools. It teaches students that racism is/was something that took place on both sides. In effect, this doctrine of 'both siderism' works to help institutions hide acts of racism and renames them as mistakes, misunderstandings or overreactions. This thinking leads students to unconsciously work to not identify racist instances and when they do, to doubt their understanding of situations as racist. Simón and Cierra when *platicando* about their experiences intuitively talked about racism but when they were asked to explicitly name racist incidents that they had experienced, they adopted the "both sides of the story" explanation and attributed the incidents to misunderstandings or their own possible overreactions.

This was one way that they had developed to cope with the insidious effects of discrimination.

Intergenerational Relationships

Our CS SFL community-based project was intergenerational (Wexler, 2011) in nature although it did center the lived experiences and knowledge(s) of youth (Cammarota & Fine, 2010; Guajardo, Guajardo, & Cantú, 2016; Tuck & Yang, 2013). During the process, researchers from the university, master's level pre-service teachers and adults from the community worked to share their knowledge(s) and experiences with youth co-researchers (Harman, Siffrinn, Mizell, & Bui, in press; Burke, Harman, Hadley, & Mizell, 2018). It was the responsibility of adult allies, whether they were adults from the community, teachers or university-based activist scholars, to lend a hand in apprenticing youth into research (Lave & Wenger, 1991; Winn & Winn, 2016). Mirra, Garcia, and Morrell (2015) wrote in regard to their work with youth that likewise they:

> Found through [their] work that adults have a crucially important role to play in facilitating the research process; that, indeed, their active mentoring and support actually bolsters youth agency. [They continue by stating that] setting young people off on a research project without access to the resources, knowledge, and relationships that adults can provide can do a disservice to YPAR by denying students the necessary tools to reap the full benefits of the process. (p. 39)

Wexler (2011) also found in her work with Native Alaskan youth that culturally appropriate dialogic conversations between elders, adults and youth fostered deeper communal relationships which nurtured youth learning and a growing sense of groundedness. This is very much in line with Holmes and González (2017) when they stated that asset pedagogies such as YPAR, and I'd argue CS SFL, are:

> Pedagogies [that] seek teaching and learning outcomes that respectfully engage with community funds of knowledge and that acknowledge that while culture can be dynamic and processual there are historically constituted reservoirs of knowledge from which communities draw. (p. 221)

CS SFL in its very nature is intergenerational. It is the co-construction of knowledge and the building of relationships that take place as youth and adults apprentice each other into their areas of knowledge that have proven to be especially powerful.

Cierra

Cierra definitely knew that she benefited from the intergenerational relationships that she developed during our time together. She also spoke about our CS SFL work as a form of apprenticeship. She stated that she learned a lot from working with us on community problem-solving and even about what was going on in the world at large. During one of our conversations, she asked why so many white people were upset with Colin Kaepernick. Cierra and I then spoke about freedom of speech, peaceful protest and police brutality. After our conversation was over, she stated, "That's what that meant [the news reports that she had seen on TV]? When they kneeled, they got sued for something... I didn't know about it. I didn't know about it until somebody told me...until you explained it to me."

Edgar

Edgar—like other youth participants—stated that one of the things that he loved about working with the CS SFL group was that he was able to learn from and with people who were older and also younger than he. During one of our first *talleres*, in response to why he wanted to continue to be part of the CS SFL program even though he was in high school, he stated that when he first arrived from Mexico, "[I got] support from my friends, from older people, like the teachers [the adults that worked within the CS SFL program], they kept pushing and like showing me new things. I would not go back and change anything. They helped me to learn. They made me stretch. They turned me into a believer. Sometimes like, I didn't want, they kept me going and learning."

Simón

Simón echoed Edgar's words when he stated in a text message that one of the things that he loved about the CS SFL project was the opportunity to learn from people of his age and older. He said, "me parecío muy interesante y genial.... bueno aprender cosas muy geniales nuevas que nos veamos cosas de un lado diferente...por que estamos trabajando con gente de diferentes edades. *(I think it is interesting and cool, it is good that we are learning new great things from different points of view...this happens because we are working with people of different ages.)*"

Edgar, Simón, and Cierra in their testimonios and later conversations all indicated an appreciation of and desire for intergenerational learning. As Holmes and González (2017) stated:

> Nesting, placing, and locating traditional Indigenous [I would also argue Black and Latine] ways of knowing and being, languages, and oral practices of intergenerational transmission at the center of a movement

of reawakening creates the possibility for contemporary reflexivity and responsiveness to the demands and immediacy of the times that are now presenting a vision of an earth straining under the unfolding grip of a worldview that is fundamentally and inherently unsustainable over the long term. All generations are needed to be in relationship with one another. (p. 220)

Adult allies need to provide support and guidance (not control) during the research process, for youth to succeed. It is through intergenerational communal, dynamic, fluid and iterative processes that youth are able to take on the mantle of researcher and policy advocate. CS SFL acknowledges and values that the languaging and cultural practices of communities are fluid and dynamic (Paris & Alim, 2017). Holmes and González (2017) when speaking about the responsibility of Western scholars (I would reframe this and say all scholars who are passionate about social justice and equity) must:

Engage in decolonizing, anticolonial self-reflection and reorientation, to recognize that the very knowledge systems they have perceived to be static, stuck, antimodern, and antiprogressive could be the very ways of knowing that hold the possibilities for collective human survival. (p. 218)

When the knowledges that youth bring with them are valued and paired with the knowledges of adult allies within and outside of their communities, youth can be equipped to take up the mantel of engaged active civic agents.

All three youth co-researchers valued working with others with different skillsets and lived experiences that helped them to hone their skills, knowledges and deepen relationships. The co-apprenticeship model, adult-youth and youth-adult helped everyone to grow in their role as active critical civic agents who can dream of a "*literacy* of pleasure and joy" (Wong & Peña, 2017, p. 118), a literacy of celebrating and nurturing the assets that have enabled our communities to thrive under oppressive systems.

A Desire to Help the Community

Over the course of the first couple of weeks of working with youth and their adult allies as part of the CS SFL projects, we always focused on examining the assets and challenges that can be found in our community(ies). As I spent time platicando y examinando their testimonios and counterstories, Cierra and Simón commented on how the CS SFL project helped them to realize ways that they could help their communities. They came to see that their newfound sense of critical literacy and civic engagement were in fact political. It is political in that it seeks to disrupt power structures, in an effort to transform the ways in which their communities have been marginalized.

Cierra

> When I'd be outside, I'd see kids getting in trouble because there wasn't anything to do. I wanted to say something because I wanted a place where kids can learn and stay out of trouble.

This was the reason that Cierra gave to a local reporter when asked why she had worked with me to open the community center in her neighborhood. She saw the center as a way of helping those who live in her community. Cierra stated that the Parkside apartment homes were and are for her, "a place where people who need a place to be, to live, can come for refuge and a fresh start." Cierra told me during one of our early conversations:

> Parkside is a community. How would I put it? I don't know, like for example, the community center, when they have fire, the person who's working there was having a funeral up there, and it was a big problem. And everybody came and you know, talked about it. Because like, we used to go out there and have fun, do homework and all that, but ever since that happened it's like, it's just nothing to do. I don't really know how to say it, but I was mad because, I don't know. I don't know how to describe it, I did, basically, I was up there because I actually liked going up there and having a person, another person, like a person to talk to. It was a place for us to be a community.

Cierra wanted to reestablish the Parkside community center so that she and others (youth and adults) could have a safe place to go. She wanted it to be a place that would help to build a sense of community, where she and her friends could do their homework and just be.

Simón

Simón felt the same way as Cierra. He desired to have places in his community where he and others could go. During the written portion of the legislative theater module in our afterschool CS SFL program, groups developed a campus redevelopment plan. Simón, the chief architect of his group's plan, included various structures such as grocery stores, clothing stores and restaurants in his neighborhood. He and Kevin, co-author of this volume, also crafted a policy statement that detailed why it was necessary to bring stores and restaurants to his neighborhood. Simón stated that his community needed those places because there wasn't anything located nearby. In order to go grocery shopping, many of the people in his neighborhood who were un(der)documented had to pay between $15 and $25 to catch a taxi or to risk driving without a license in order to shop in surrounding communities. These are some of the things that Simón and others felt were missing from their neighborhoods: a medical center, bike trails/racks, swimming pool, trees, outdoor classrooms, parks and soccer fields among other things.

Simón, Edgar and Cierra were emphatic about the ways they wanted to help their communities to have access to resources that would be of benefit to them. Through the CS SFL civic engagement, they deepened their connection to home and school neighborhoods (Ardoin, Castrechini, & Hofstedt, 2014). As Manzo and Perkins (2006) describe: "people are motivated to seek, stay in, protect, and improve places that are meaningful to them" (p. 347). Throughout all of our conversations, my youth co-researchers consistently talked about the importance of community in their lives. Their growing awareness of the power of their voices and ideas helped them begin to realize that they could have a hand in helping their communities to build on its assets. They also showed a growing critical awareness of how language and other semiotic resources could be harnessed to make changes in their lives. While presenting at a national linguistics conference, Simon stated that he learned from the CS SFL program how power and social action rests not only in words, but also in use of pictures, designs and drama.

Discussion

This chapter has focused on the importance of not only listening to the testimonios of youth but also recognizing that their testimonios when proactively listened to can lead to positive changes in their lives and the lives of their communities. Often in our data-driven world, the "stories" or lived-experiences of our students aren't centered or even taken into consideration when decisions are made. Jason, by centering his youth co-participants' testimonios, shifted from the traditional roles of researcher and researched in university projects and instead co-constructed knowledge through a process of collaborative data collection, dialog and analysis. Additionally, his approach decentered hegemonic ways of understanding how educational research should be carried out (Huber, 2012; Alemán, 2017). Lindsay Pérez Huber (2012) states that *testimonios* are powerful because they (a) foreground injustices caused by oppression, (b) challenge whiteness ideologies, (c) value minoritized community knowledge(s), (d) recognize the power of human collectivity and (e) center a focus on racial and social justice.

Within the framework of CS SFL, the theory and praxis of SFL validated and served as impetus for an equity and civic engagement project where minoritized students "usurped dominant genres [and ways of creating knowledge] to create a discursive third space in which their subaltern voices/[testimonios] pushed back against negative social positioning of their lived experiences and communities" (Khote & Tian, 2019, p. 10). Within this new space, they also spoke of the joys of their communities. The knowledges and assets that made them smile, kept their families and communities strong and gave them hope.

The testimonios of Jason's co-researchers decentered the deficit discourses which too often frame their communities and their own lives. Instead, it provided us with deep insights into the strength and resilience of our youth members and together how they could address the challenges and obstacles they face on a daily basis.

Cierra's testimonio showed us that although she was reticent to talk about racism, she was very cognizant of how it was impacting her educational present and could possibly impact her future hopes and dreams. She was also very aware that she needed and wanted to be mentored or apprenticed into critical ways of examining the world around her. As she put it, "we need teachers who can help us no matter!" In our many conversations, there was always the understanding that for Cierra, teachers were not just those found in school buildings but also the adults with whom she interacted that were willing to listen to, care for and guide her. Simón and Edgar were very similar to Cierra in many ways. They also appreciated and valued the work that they did with people younger than them and also older. Additionally, they valued the variety of ideas and experiences that they interacted with through the CS SFL project.

The CS SFL framework provided the tools and also a discursive third space that youth used to explicitly deconstruct and examine linguistic and institutional ideologies. It also centered their experiences, lives and knowledges as normal and valuable. It did not compare their experiences to those of white middle and upper-middle class people in order to ascertain if they were of value or not. This framework also did not constrict their knowledge production to approved Eurocentric metrics. CS SFL allowed them to use a great many semiotic resources that they had at their disposal to produce knowledge. Their testimonios came to me as pictures, models, songs, poetry, bodily movements and text messages among various other modes.

CS SFL allowed them to grow as active critical civic agents who can deconstruct and produce multimodal text. Furthermore, the CS SFL program helped them to access a wide range of semiotic resources to develop and expand upon their testimonios.

Delpit (2006) urged everyone that works with minoritized students to help them to become critical consumers and producers of knowledge so that they don't "simply [become] the grease that keeps the institutions which orchestrate [their] oppression running smoothly" (p. 19). This means that we must help them to critically tell their stories. We must learn to center and value non-dominant ways of producing knowledge. It is only by willingly becoming their co-participants, co-researchers and co-sharers of personal knowledges, insights and experiences, that we can help them and ourselves to find reflections of ourselves in testimonios as windows, mirrors and sliding glass doors (Bishop, 1990).

As more and more bilingual and bi-dialectical children enter our schools, they need healthy ways of reflecting on their own experiences, connecting with others and understanding that they are not alone. Through the use of a LatCrit lens, this study has shown that *testimonios* in conjunction with CS SFL offered Jason and his youth co-researchers, and hopefully you the reader with, opportunities to see not only how elements of our life experiences are shared by others, but also how others have navigated, thrived and found joy in the educational spaces in which we find ourselves as we work to become active producers of critical literacy.

Praxis

The following discussion questions and prompts are designed to support readers in forming and deepening relationships in collaborative research groups in school or informal contexts:

1. What stories of strength or the overcoming of hardship have been passed down through your family or friendship group(s)?
2. What accounts of joy in the face of adversity have helped you to grow?
3. Work to begin to share your history and your stories with your class or participants in your program. If you want them to open themselves up to you, you must also humanize yourself to them. (See Paris 2011; Paris & Winn, 2013)
4. Write your own counter story or testimonio and share it with your students.
5. Once you have developed a trusting relationship with your students, ask them to write their own counterstories or testimonios or those of their families.

Notes

1 In the tradition of many Critical Race Theory scholars/researchers (Crenshaw, 1988; Taylor, Gillborn, & Ladson-Billings, 2016), I have purposefully chosen to not capitalize white as a way of decentering whiteness and thus centering the lives and experiences of people of color broadly speaking.
2 I have chosen to use the term Latine instead of the original term Latino in this manuscript as one way of breaking down the binary that may be produced by using the term, Latino. Latino generally implies that one is either male (Latino) or female (Latina). Latine is used to express that within the community of those who identify culturally, linguistically or otherwise with those who reside in Latin America there exist numerous ways of identifying other than as simply male or female. Some Spanish speakers in Latin America now use this term instead of Latinx as it is pronounceable in Spanish, whereas Latinx isn't.

3 Languaging refers to the "dynamic, never-ending process of using language to make making" (Swain, 2006, p. 96).
4 All names are pseudonyms unless the youth and their parent(s) decided they wanted to use their real names. Edgar's name is not a pseudonym as he wanted to be a contributing author in this book.
5 Cassie Louise Lightfoot the eight-year-old protagonist has a dream to be free to go wherever she wants in 1939 Harlem, New York. One night as she and her family are on "tar beach," the rooftop of her family's Harlem apartment building, she begins to dream. She is able to fly high about various places in New York and dreams of changing things so that race is no longer an issue.
6 This refers to an immigration center/jail where he was kept. It is referred to as the refrigerator or freezer because the temperature is intentionally kept low.

References

Alemán, S. M. (2017). Testimonio as praxis for a reimagined journalism model and pedagogy. In D. Delgado Bernal, R. Burciaga, & J. Flores Carmona (Eds.) *Chicana/Latina testimonies and pedagogical, methodological, and activist approaches to social justice* (pp. 137–155). London, UK: Routledge.
Ardoin, N., Castrechini, S., & Hofstedt, M. (2014). Youth-community-university partnerships and sense of place: Two case studies of youth participatory action research. *Children Geographies, 12*(4). 479–496. doi:10.1080/14733285.2013.827872
Baszile, D. T. (2015). Rhetorical revolution: Critical race counterstorytelling and the abolition of White democracy. *Qualitative Inquiry, 21*(3), 239–249.
Bernal, D. D. (2002). Critical race theory, Latino critical theory, and critical raced-gendered epistemologies: Recognizing students of color as holders and creators of knowledge. *Qualitative Inquiry, 8*(1), 105–126.
Bernal, D. D., & Villalpando, O. (2002). An apartheid of knowledge in academia: The struggle over the 'legitimate' knowledge of faculty of color. *Equity & Excellence in Education, 35*(2), 169–180. doi:10.1080/713845282.
Beverly, J. (2000). Testimonio, subalternity, and narrative authority. In N. K. Denzin, & Y. S. Lincoln (Eds.) *Handbook of qualitative research* (pp. 555–565). Thousand Oaks, CA: SAGE.
Bishop, R. S. (1990). Mirrors, windows, and sliding glass doors. *Perspectives, 6*(3), ix–xi.
Burke, K. J., Harman, R., Hadley, H. L., & Mizell, J. D. (2018). 'I could not believe that would happen': Challenges and opportunities in a critical, project-based clinical experience. *The New Educator, 14*(3), 212–230.
Cammarota, J., & Fine, M. (2010). *Revolutionizing education: Youth participatory action research in motion.* New York, NY: Routledge.
Cook, D. A., & Dixson, A. D. (2013). Writing critical race theory and method: A composite counterstory on the experiences of black teachers in New Orleans post-Katrina. *International Journal of Qualitative Studies in Education, 26*(10), 1238–1258. doi:10.1080/09518398.2012.731531.
Crenshaw, K., Gotanda, N., Peller, G., & Thomas, N. (Eds.). (1995). *Critical race theory: The key writings that formed the movement.* New York, NY: The New Press.
Del Vecchio, D., Toomey, N., & Tuck, E. (2017). Placing photovoice: Participatory action research with undocumented migrant youth in the Hudson Valley. *Critical Questions in Education, 8*(4), 358–376.

Delgado, R., & Stefancic, J. (2000). *Critical race theory: The cutting edge*. Philadelphia, PA: Temple University Press.

Delpit, L. (2006). *Other people's children: Cultural conflict in the classroom*. New York, NY: The New Press.

Eggins, S. (2004). *Introduction to systemic functional linguistics*. New York, NY: A&C Black.

Esposito, N. (2001). From meaning to meaning: The influence of translation techniques on non-English focus group research. *Qualitative Health Research, 11*(3), 568–579.

Fierros, C. O., & Delgado Bernal, D. (2016). Vamos a platicar: The contours of pláticas as Chicana/Latina feminist methodology. *Chicana/Latina Studies, 15*(2), 98–121.

Fien, J. (s.f.). Indigenous knowledge & sustainability. Accessed June 23, 2019, Obtenido de Teaching and learning for a sustainable future: http://www.unesco.org/education/tlsf/mods/theme_c/mod11.html

Flores Carmona, J. (2014). Cutting out their tongues: Mujeres' testimonios and the Malintzin researcher. *Journal of Latino/Latin American Studies, 6*(2), 113–124.

Flores Carmona, J., Hamzeh, M., Bejarano, C., & Hernández Sánchez, M. E. (2018). Pláticas~testimonios: Practicing methodological borderlands for solidarity and resilience in academia. *Chicana/Latina Studies: The Journal of Mujeres Activas en Letras y Cambio Social, 18*(1), 30–52.

Georgia, U. S. (2010, October 13). *Regents Adopt New Policies on Undocumented Students*. Retrieved March 15, 2019, from Communications The central communications/public information operation for the USG: https://www.usg.edu/news/release/regents_adopt_new_policies_on_undocumented_students

Gramsci, A. (2005). *Selections from prison notebooks*. (Q. H. Smith, Ed.) London: Lawrence and Wishart.

Guajardo, F., & Guajardo, M. (2013). The power of plática. *Reflectios: A Journal of Public Rhetoric, Civic Writing, and Service Learning, 13*(1), 159–164.

Guajardo, F., Guajardo, M., & Cantú, M. (2016). Where are they now? An intergenerational conversation on the work of the Llano Grande center for research and development. In S. Greene, K. Burke, & M. McKenna (Eds.) *Youth voices, public spaces, and civic engagement* (pp. 169–185). New York, NY: Routledge.

Harman, R., Siffrinn, N. E., Mizell, J. D., & Bui, K. (in press,). Promoting reflection literacy in pre-service language teacher education through critical praxis with multilingual youth. In L. Alatriste, & C. Crosby (Eds.) *Second language writing across PK16 contexts; Intersections of teaching, learning, and development*. Ann Arbor, MI: University of Michigan Press.

Harper, S. R., Patton, L. D., & Wooden, O. S. (2009). Access and equity for African American students in higher education: A critical race historical analysis of policy efforts. *Journal of Higher Education, 80*(4), 389–414.

Heilbrun, A., Cornell, D., & Konold, T. (2018). Authoritative school climate and suspension rates in middle schools: Implications for reducing the racial disparity in school discipline. *Journal of School Violence, 17*(3), 324–338,. doi:10.1080/15388220.2017.1368395

Holmes, A., & González, N. (2017). Finding sustenance: An indigenous relational pedagogy. In D. Paris, & H. Alim (Eds.) *Culturally sustaining pedagogies: Teaching and learning for justice in a changing world* (pp. 207–224). New York, NY: Teachers College Press.

Huber, L. P. (2012). Testimonio as LatCrit methodolgy in education. In S. Delamont (Ed.) *Handbook of qualitative research in education* (pp. 377–390). Cheltenham, UK: Edward Elgar Publishing.

Hurston, Z. N. (1942). *Dust tracks on a road*. New York, NY: Arno Press.

Khote, N., & Tian, Z. (2019). Translanguaging in culturally sustaining systemic functional linguistics. *Translation and Translanguaging in Multilingual Contexts, 5*(1), 5–28.

Kubota, R. (2019). Confronting Epistemological Racism, Decolonizing Scholarly Knowledge: Race and Gender in Applied Linguistics. *Applied Linguistics*, 1-22. doi:10.1093/applin/amz033

Lave, J., & Wenger, E. (1991). *Situated learning: Legitimate peripheral participation*. Cambridge, MA: Cambridge University Press.

Manzo, L., & C. Perkins. (2006). Finding common ground: The importance of place attachment to community participation and planning. *Journal of Planning Literature, 20*(4), 335–349.

Menchú, R. (2018). In *Funk & Wagnalls New World Encyclopedia (p. 1)*. Retrieved June 31, 2019, from http://search.ebscohost.com.proxy-remote.galib.uga.edu/login.aspx?direct=true&db=funk&AN=me084250&site=eds-live

Menchú-Tum, R., & Gugelberger, G. M. (1998). Remembering: The post-testimonio memoirs of Rigoberta Menchú Tum. *Latin American Perspectives, 25*(6), 62–68.

Mirra, N., Garcia, A., & Morrell, E. (2015). *Doing youth participatory action research: Transforming inquiry with researchers, educators, and students*. New York, NY: Routledge.

Morris, M. (2016). *Pushout: The criminalization of Black girls in schools*. New York, NY. The New Press.

Orelus, P. W. (2018). Can subaltern professors speak?: examining micro-aggressions and lack of inclusion in the academy. *Qualitative Research Journal*, 169–179. doi:10.1108/QRJ-D-17-00057.

Paris, D. (2011). 'A friend who understand fully': Notes on humanizing research in a multiethnic youth community. *International Journal of Qualitative Studies in Education, 24*(2), 137–149.

Paris, D., & Alim, H. S. (2017). *Culturally sustaining pedagogies : Teaching and learning for justice in a changing world*. New York, NY: Teachers College Press.

Paris, D., & Winn, M. T. (2013). *Humanizing research: Decolonizing qualitative inquiry with youth and communities*. Thousand Oaks, CA: SAGE.

Pérez-Huber, L. (2012). Testimonio as LatCrit methodology in education. In S. Delamont (Ed.) *Handbook of Qualitative Research in Education*. (p. 377). Cheltenham, UK: Edward Elgar.

Pérez Rhym, M. (2017). Buscando la Forma: How Latinx Mothers Navigate Parental Support Gaps in New Latino Diaspora Schools (Doctoral dissertation, University of Georgia). Athens, Georgia, U.S.A.

Ringgold, F. (1991). *Tar beach*. New York, NY: Crown.

Rodriguez, T. L. (2011). Stories of self, stories of practice: Enacting a vision of socially just pedagogy for Latino youth. *Teaching Education, 22*(3), 239–254.

Smith, H. L., Flores, B. B., & González, D. A. (2015). Exploring the traditions of Latino children's literature: Beyond tokenism to transformation. In E. R. Clark, B. B. Flores, H. L. Smith, & D. A. González (Eds.) *Multicultural literature for Latino bilingual children: Their words, their worlds* (pp. 25–48). Lanham, MD: Rowman Littlefield.

Stefancic, J. (1997). Latino and Latina critical theory: An annotated bibliography. *California Law Review, 85*(5), 423–498.

Stoll, D. (2008). *Rigoberta Menchú and the story of all poor Guatemalans*. Boulder, CO: Westview.

Swain, M. (2006). Languaging, agency and collaboration in advanced language proficiency. In H. Byrnes, *Advanced language learning: The contribution of Halliday and Vygotsky* (pp. 95–108). London: Continuum.

Tafari, D. N. (2018). 'Whose world is this?': A composite counterstory of Black male elementary school teachers as hip-hop otherfathers. *The Urban Review, 50*(5), 795–817.

Taylor, E., Gillborn, D., & Ladson-Billings, G. (2016). *Foundations of critical race theory in education.* New York, NY: Routledge.

Teeger, C. (2015). 'Both sides of the story' history education in post-apartheid South Africa. *American Sociological Review, 80*(6), 1175–1200.

Tuck, E., & Yang, K. W. (2013). *Youth resistance research and theories of change. Routledge.* New York, NY: Routledge.

University System of Georgia. (2010, October 13). Regents Adopt New Policies on Undocumented Students. Retrieved March 15, 2019, from Communications The central communications/public information operation for the USG: https://www.usg.edu/news/release/regents_adopt_new_policies_on_undocumented_students

Wallace, J. M., Goodkind, S., Wallace, C. M., & Bachman, J. G. (2008). Racial, ethnic, and gender differences in school discipline among U.S. high school students: 1991-2005. *The Negro Educational Review, 59*(1-2), 47–62.

Weiss, B. (2018, January 11). *The Trump administration has ended protections for immigrants from 4 countries—here's when they will have to leave the US.* Retrieved April 21, 2019, from https://www.businessinsider.com/trump-has-ended-temporary-protection-status-for-4-countries-2018-1

Welsh, R. O., & Little, S. (2018). The school discipline dilemma: A comprehensive review of disparities and alternative approaches. *Review of Educational Research, 88*(5), 752–794.

Wexler, L. (2011). Intergenerational dialogue exchange and action: Introducing a community-based participatory approach to connect youth, adults and elders in an Alaskan Native community. *International Journal of Qualitative Methods, 10*(3), 248–264.

Winn, L.T., & Winn, M.T. (2016). 'We want this to be owned by you': The promise and perils of youth participatory action research. In S. Greene, K. J. Burke, & M. K. McKenna (Eds.) *Youth voices, literacies, and civic engagement* (pp. 111–130). New York, NY: Routledge.

Wong, C., & Peña, C. (2017). Policing and performing culture: Rethinking 'culture' and the role of the arts in culturally sustaining pedagogies. In D. Paris, & H. S. Alim (Eds.) *Culturally sustaining pedagogies: Teaching and learning for justice in a changing world* (pp. 117–140). New York, NY: Teachers College Press.

Yancy, G. (2008). *Black bodies, white gazes: The continuing significance of race in America.* Lanham, MD: Rowman & Littlefield.

PRELUDE TO CHAPTER 4

Visual and Spatial Modalities

Chapter 3 provided readers with an understanding of the lived testimonios, deep insights and collaborative dreams of participants in our CS SFL programs. Chapter 4 explores the affordances of place making, mapping, neighborhood walking and environmental design in our CS SFL programs. Within this approach to youth programs, design is conceptualized as the process in which resources and patterns from multiple modes are made available to youth to creatively remix new meanings for their social, civic and academic purposes. According to Hasan (2011), such contributions of new knowledge to our society are as a key civic right of all citizens.

In conceptualizing the function of design, researchers focus on two primary elements of mode and medium (Bezemer & Kress, 2016; Cimasko & Shin, 2017). A mode is a channel of communication that is culturally ratified as a meaning-making set of signs (e.g., writing, mapping, drawing, dancing); and it has a configuration of available resources it may share with similar modes. For example, the mode of mapping a geographical area and of constructing scaled 3D models of a building to go into that space share certain modal resources (e.g., sketching, multimodal text, mathematical symbols); similarly, speech and writing share certain modal resources such as lexis, grammar and text types. Configurations of modes will differ according to the medium of communication. In our work, youth engaged in mapping a neighborhood to share with community members and learned to enact a set of discourse practices related to surveying, sketching and scaling that might be seen as overly specialized in a casual walking around the neighborhood. The patterned coupling of modes, in other words, differs according to the social purpose, audience and medium.

In this section of the book, we share our work on spatial and visual modes with the hope that you can also reflect on the rich and sustainable ways that youth engage with these spaces and how you can incorporate these modes into your teaching or community context. As Derr, Chawla, and Mintzer (2018) state: "Participatory processes with young people cultivate citizens who know how to work collaboratively to create a more sustainable future" (p. 9). Ultimately, what is found through this work is that youth benefit not only from thinking deeply about local, contextual and entrenched problems, but also from a structured process that is intergenerational (i.e., involving youth and adults of different ages) and linked to different modal and linguistic affordances that support community problem-solving and civic agency (e.g., writing, community dialogue, performance, photography, etc.). The immersion in spatial, visual, verbal and actional resources expands dialogic exchanges among participants in our programs and this extends outward to their engagement in other academic, intellectual and artistic pursuits.

References

Bezemer, J. J., & Kress, G. R. (2016). *Multimodality, learning and communication: A social semiotic frame*. London, UK: Routledge.

Cimasko, T., & Shin, D. (2017). Multimodal resemiotization and authorial agency in an L2 writing classroom. *Written Communication, 34*(4), 387–413.

Derr, V., Chawla, L., & Mintzer, M. (2018). *Placemaking with children and youth: Participatory practices for planning sustainable communities*. New York, NY: New Village Press.

Hasan, R. (2011). *Language and education: Learning and teaching in society*. London, UK: Equinox.

4

CS SFL PRAXIS: MAPPING AND DESIGNING

Khanh Bui and Kevin J. Burke

Why maps? Or, in other words, among the myriad options for thinking about space with kids, what is it about cartographic work that might suggest interesting—new, thoughtful, radical—orientations to the world? One answer is embedded below in thinking about how spaces get created and bounded, eventually, by official maps, their histories and attendant narratives. Another answer comes from Halliday who noted that "language provides members of discourse communities with a system of choices to communicate meaning" (Harman, 2018, p. 4). Thinking about the organizing principles of Systemic Functional Linguistics (SFL), we can return to notions of the field (the topic or activity sequence), the tenor (relationships with people) and the mode (how is this topic, in relationship, being organized and talked about?). In this case, we can think, very clearly, about the map as the mode: In order to build the field about the spaces and places of a neighborhood, school, community, city, world, we want to orient ourselves to maps—which are, of course, orienting devices themselves. We might choose more traditional approaches: We could survey youth about their feelings about the grounds around their schools; we could ask them to write narratives about the boundaries of their neighborhoods; we could co-construct spoken word poems about the meaning of community and its limits. In fact we've done all of these things, but the point is that, in different modes, the youth and adults have access to different information. Maps, in particular, allow kids to do interesting work about and around space in reimagining power geometries.

If we're tasked, then, with helping youth think about the ways in which they might alter a space—or a place, depending on how familiar they are with it—then we might frame the discourse through a familiar mode: the map. Kids see maps all the time. Increasingly this is true on phones as they navigate around—perhaps

also in relation to games that are immersive, like Pokemon Go!—and generations raised in immersive technologies such as these might actually see maps as
much more fluid than their predecessors for whom maps mostly sat on walls, or
spring loaded at the front of classrooms, to be pulled down on the odd geography
quiz day. The point being: Where we used to plot on maps, kids often, now, see
themselves as glowing, blinking dots on them which reorient to them as they
move through a space. This isn't to suggest that maps are no longer determina-
tive and static (and colonializing in what they enshrine and ignore), but it is a
way of saying that youth are used to maps changing and shifting based on their
experiences. We'd do well to harness this reality to do new things.

If we think of the map as a semiotic resource for reengineering the lived
experience of a place for youth—who might turn an unfamiliar space into a
place by creating their own maps—then we get at the heart of the work of both
CS SFL and critical geographic studies: the creation of new knowledge. This,
of course, is the work of reflection literacy where "learners...see themselves as
capable of producing new knowledge and not just learning what others present
for them to take up" (Schleppegrell & Moore, 2018, p. 25). In this case, if we
approach youth with the notion that they can be movers of social policy, one
way to direct that movement is through the literal remapping, the reshaping, of
the spaces that affect them in their lives. Below we share examples of pedagogies, using mapping in various forms, to argue for this practice as a vital mode
through which youth can develop capacity in action literacy driving toward the
change available in reflection literacy (Hasan, 2011).

Walking Spaces and Places

One of the central dilemmas we face in our work with youth lies in their dis-
comfort in official spaces. That is: Often when we're in research and artistic
situations with kids, and particularly minoritized kids, we're in institutionalized
environments. Usually this means we're in schools or museums, but also community centers. Because of the shared histories many of our youth have in these
kinds of environments—mostly they're experienced as unwelcoming or punitive
in their orientation to kids' bodies—we have to work with youth to think about
how we might reconceptualize the various spaces of their lives in order to better
understand how they might re-design solutions to the problems they identify in
their communities.

Stuart Aitken, in his work, *Geographies of Young People: The Morally Contested
Spaces of Identity* (2001) suggests that when we attend to the particular spaces
experienced—and created—by youth, we must account for the ways in which:

> What is produced for young people are everyday lives that are spatially
> circumscribed by powerful adults who, as often as not, fail to recognize

the multiple ways children and teenagers shape their political identities and the scale of the day-to-day. (p. 22)

Rather simply put, kids are subject (as are adults of course) to "power geometries" that "refract and reflect global economic processes" (p. 136) which seek to produce, most often in reference to kids and particularly kids in schools, docile bodies first, and perhaps later—although maybe not always—fruitful minds. The point of this chapter, and in relation to the larger volume here, although, is that there are ways in which kids navigate the spaces of their lives—inhabiting them, inhibited by them, interpreting them, remaking them, etc.—that we might creatively access for the sake of driving educational and social change to the benefit of and in concert with youth-as-advocates-for-change. And one mode for beginning discussions about the use of space is through mapping.

Mapping, and the production of maps, as with other technologies for making meaning contains "referents to systems of power-knowledge. By what they depict and what they omit—the presences and absences—maps represent particular worldviews and structures of knowledge" (Aitken, 2001, p. 49). Indeed, in his research with upper elementary school students, Nespor (1997) found that when asked to map their spaces—rather than to interpret maps already made of the spaces in their lives, importantly—"kids focused on spaces that could be reworked for their own uses" (p. 117). In order to make sense of this reworking, Nespor asked youth to map their neighborhoods, and found that "kids' relations with a school and with the social and material spaces they move through, are products of their ongoing histories and geographies" (p. 94) which might, in some ways, feel obvious. But getting kids to discuss those histories, those geographies, in order to account for the sorts of power geometries that are often quietly shaping their schooled, neighborhood and community lives is often tricky. Our argument here, as in other places in the book, is that multiple affordances of art can help unlock interesting discussions and inquiry with youth about community—in this case, spatial—change. And particularly, that asking kids to work with—that is: create, alter, co-construct and reflect on—localized maps can not only reshape our visions of space, but also provide entry into deeper understanding of what kids do to space, and what spaces do for and to kids.

To provide us with a brief background on how these questions of spatiality are conceptualized, we need to play a bit in theories of geography, in order to get our terms straight (or as straight as is possible in a necessarily abstract and amorphous field). Depending on how you read the literature, you will most likely run into varying accounts of *space* and *place*. Along the way it's worth thinking about notions of landscape as well, for the sake of negative definition (x is not this and so it might be *that,* in other words). Always it's worth keeping in mind that these definitions are partial and often overlap. For now, we can think of these definitions as heuristics: helpful beginning guides to build our conversation.

For Cresswell (2004) landscape "is an intensely visual idea. In most definitions of landscape the viewer is outside of it" (p. 10) adding, in a perhaps helpful way, "we do not live in landscapes—we look at them" (p. 11). We might pause here to consider the ways in which adults tend to survey the landscape of the lived existences of youth; most often we look on from the outside either baffled by the process and scale of youth play, or, more likely, seeking to circumscribe its possibilities out of a sense of decorum, fear or through pleas to safety and discipline.

Space and place are different from landscape in that they are closer in. They are lived rather than looked at, in essence. Indeed, in some ways they are used interchangeably. Cresswell, again, argues that "space is a more abstract concept of place" where "places have space between them" adding, from Tuan (1979) that we might "think of space as that which allows movement" where place is "pause" (p. 8). Blundell (2016) similarly thinks of a process by which spaces become places for people "through associations with human meaning" (p. 46). We could consider the way in which historical markers, along highways, are meant to induce pauses—for a particular kind of person, these are inducements to stop; invitations to fix a point in a landscape; to elide passing through a space, and pause in a place that has come to mean through the implied historicity of a particular spot, and by necessity, the lack of significance of various spots in the surround.

A quick turn to postmodern geographies is helpful here. Soja (1989) suggests that attending to "an instrumental cartography of power and social control" is vital as "a more acute way of seeing how space hides consequences from us" (p. 63). Of course one way to attend to power is through, well, cartography, in thinking of the ways in which maps create, encode and reinforce narratives of the world. Maps have long been tools of colonialism (Katz, 2005; Pacheco & Velez, 2009), imprinting a settler's gaze and (literal) impression into and onto land (and water!) and people without consideration of the many alternative understandings of place that might otherwise emerge through dialog rather than, say, conquest. At the same time, although, counter-mapping—or for Katz, "countertopographies"—offers opportunities for different orientations to arise, different stories to emerge about experiences with spaces and places, most especially, for our purposes, through the recreation of maps from below—in this case, by youth.

Literat (2013) chronicles various modes of participatory counter-mapping with youth, focusing in on the ways in which youth in an afterschool program were able to filigree existing maps with new orientations; that is: How might youth, given officialized maps, tell different kinds of narratives about place? What emerges is a sense from the researcher that (a) media representations heavily influence youth perceptions of safety and comfort and (b) geographic isolation, tied to transportation issues, is a central experience of many urban youth. As safety and comfort in a given space on a map are directly tied to familiarity with a place, a lack of transportation—in this case public transportation—effectively embeds stereotypes of different groups, as manifest in corporate media, in youth perceptions of a city. Everything that isn't familiar is landscape, looked at through lenses colored by images of shootings, gang activity or danger. Akom, Shah, and Nakai (2014) used GIS mapping with youth to think about environmental and community health with a focus on youth learning tools of inquiry (p. 97) but especially with a sense that "youth themselves were often the individuals who have the most current and accurate understanding of race, space, place and waste in [a] neighborhood" (p. 99). The idea is that maps, as tools of inquiry—whether modified or wholly created—provide youth, who have a localized knowledge often missed by adults, different tools for telling stories about the presence and absence of resources. This chapter, in turn, illuminates a few projects where maps, and community walks, allowed for new and different orientations to space—turning, often, landscape into place for participants.

Mapping Neighborhoods

For the past decade, across a number of contexts, Kevin has worked with youth both in school and out of school to imagine and pursue community change. This work is rooted in youth participatory action research which, like all activist research traditions, is "committed to a set of disciplined material practices that produce," hopefully, "radical, democratizing transformations in the civic sphere" most often achieved through "dialogue, participatory decision-making, inclusive democratic deliberation, and the maximal participation and representation of all relevant parties" (Denzin & Lincoln, 2011, p. 21). Ultimately products matter, but the process of the work, particularly with youth, is aimed at "developing the skills and capacities of the community participants through the research process" (Brydon-Miller, Kral, Maguire, Noffke, & Sabhlok, 2011, p. 390). Our focus, then, when beginning our work with youth—usually in late middle through high school—lies in helping them elucidate their notions of community (its meanings, boundaries, possibilities and limitations). After introductions, often focused on family stories tied to our names, we send youth off in small groups—most often with undergraduate or graduate student co-researchers—with paper, and art supplies, and ask them to "map their neighborhoods." What we get, when we reconvene as a large group, often varies immensely. Some youth take the task as literally as one might imagine, seeking to reproduce the form of maps they've encountered in their lives, with a verisimilitude that we think comes from practices in schools related to mapping as a process of reproduction and not much else (e.g., 'color x country y color' and so forth). In other cases we get highly stylized pictures, renderings not so much of streets and rivers, but of flashpoints for stories: the important houses that mark their walks home; places where family gathers in public; nodes of community pride and fear. What is most illuminating, and what drives the discussion among adults and youth, throughout and after the exercise is the reality that—unsurprising in practice, but still useful from the standpoint of lived *places* as political conduits to power—the youth-drawn neighborhoods never match official maps. That is: The lived neighborhoods of youth never mime the boundaries of officialized names and contour lines. In that sense, what we might first note, is that for kids, neighborhoods are fluid, and most often they reflect a sense of play—where are the playgrounds to which I have access?—family—whose spaces do I have access to?—and memory—this happened here, and is vital to my understanding of neighborhood.

Intriguing, as well, is that the vast majority of our youth who in these projects tend to be youth of color from various socioeconomic backgrounds, but predominantly in lower income strata, nearly never include their schools in neighborhood drawings. These are data by omission, and in some cases this is just about physical proximity mixed with school choice policies implemented by states: A lot of our youth just don't attend their neighborhood schools if they even exist anymore. More to the point, although: Schools have been, for our youth, mostly disconnected from the experience of civic life. They aren't places that signify care or joy. They are often punitive spaces, necessary evils to be escaped at the end of the day, week or year. An example might help here: Early in our work in a mid-sized town in the Midwest, two young men recounted, at the beginning of their school year, the principal gathering the student body for an assembly. This tradition, of itself, isn't particularly noteworthy: Here is a welcome to the new year from the leader of the school. However, the content of the event was focused entirely on student test scores. The principal made it clear—and this was at the end of No Child Left Behind, segueing into Race to the Top—that if student test scores didn't improve, she would lose her job. She hoped that they wouldn't allow that to happen. The boys we worked with, who attended that school, wore that burden heavily. They weren't particularly strong students by traditional measures although they were deeply quiet, empathetic and introspective kids, struggling with homelessness for most of our time together, and concerned, in their hearts, that they were on their way to ruining an adult's life. This isn't a chapter about the various un/intentional evils of high stakes testing, standardization and punitive faculty evaluation—just as it's not necessarily *not* a chapter about that—and we certainly don't mean to impugn the motives of dedicated educators most often stuck in the vice of a system badly distorted by priorities that miss the real cause of student struggle. Rather, we mention this episode because, when the boys drew their neighborhoods, they were careful to let us know that they weren't including their school. Whatever the physical boundaries of the place, the boys saw their public school as outside the scope of community, of home. This is important, we think, and we were only able to connect the experience of the assembly with their disconnect from school-as-community-actor through the maps they drew for us.

Walking Tours

One of the difficulties we had, early in our work with youth trying to understand the ways in which they wanted to think about community change came through failed pedagogy. At the front end of the research, with colleagues in the Midwest, Kevin embarked on a simple, eight-week photovoice project, run under the auspices of a neighborhood-resource organization with the aim of eliciting things youth loved about their neighborhoods and things they would want to change. And so, naively, we gathered about a half dozen middle school kids, set up a one-session lesson in photographic methods and asked them to come back the next session, a week later, with 24 pictures: 12 representing what they loved and 12 representing what they'd change. Disposable cameras in hand, the kids dispersed into a slushy early-afternoon Saturday and we congratulated ourselves on pulling together this really interesting opportunity for kids to express themselves through pictures. You might imagine where this is going. The next week we had kids back with us and we had half-filled cameras—if the kids had remembered the cameras at all. When we asked our subjects—which is how we conceived of them at that point—to discuss the pictures they'd taken, youth were ready to talk about what they'd represented in their photos—as yet undeveloped—as assets in their communities. These were thoughtful kids: They loved the library; the vibrancy of the downtown area; parks near their houses; family heirlooms on porches. The grinding halt came when we asked them to discuss what they'd taken pictures of that they wanted to change. No one had pictures to document it on the film in their cameras. And no one had anything to say.

Faced with a *long* uncomfortable silence, and a great deal of time to fill with kids on a Saturday, we engineered some activities and huddled, after the kids had left, to think about what had happened, how we'd failed. What we realized, of course, is that good activist—youth—research is like good pedagogy: It requires relationships rooted in trust and shared experience. The kids didn't share what they saw as holes in their communities because they didn't know us well enough to trust in our capacity to empathize rather than sensationalize the failings of their communities. So we adjusted. The first thing we did is ask them, for the subsequent session, to come with their cameras and—by a stroke of luck and a break in the Indiana weather this was doable in January—comfortable shoes. And we went on a tour of the city with them. They guided us on the streets of their city; they took us on shortcuts through fields we'd never noticed before; we weaved on and off sidewalks broken by tree roots and decades of neglect; they took us to the river to watch the rapids forming from the recent snowmelt and to a park to hang upside down on playground equipment. Along the way they told us about how violence at their schools worried them as they saw it spilling into their neighborhoods; they talked about parents shattered by addiction and peers recruited by gangs. They talked about the restorative power of the churches in their communities and the shock of realizing that their parents had hidden a need to use food stamps as a way to keep the family afloat. And they led us. We followed, and they took pictures of the things that they wanted to change: neglected infrastructure; clear evidence of homelessness—and systemic injustice; tacit racial dividing lines. In short, they presented a vulnerability that we otherwise wouldn't have found had we not wandered their spaces with them.

The connection to maps is, perhaps, a bit too clear here. The youth could have drawn us maps of their communities—in fact, they did!—but for us to get a feel for their spaces, to understand how they moved in the city—and where, for example, they weren't allowed to go because of parents' fears of violence—we had to tag along. The walking tours, youth led, have become a staple of our work since that day and although we run it differently in Georgia than we might in Indiana—as you'll see in the next section—the same idea remains: Kids move through spaces differently than we would as adults, and in order to get a sense for the physical realities of their lives we would do well to trail them on their, well, trails, because youth never follow gridlines in this experience. We are always cutting through neglected cemeteries, hopping ill-used fences, digging up forgotten historical markers and wondering aloud why boundaries are put in place by the powers that be. In short, we are, with the youth, remapping a neighborhood, a city, through our informal tours.

Narrative Mapping of a School

In a different state and context, in Georgia and in an afterschool program, the mapping and walking with youth took on a different flavor and orientation. Khanh Bui shares this scenario and its purpose to highlight how this work can be taken up in different contexts and for a range of purposes. In 2017 and 2018, we developed a CS SFL afterschool program in a middle school in northeastern Georgia. This program enabled youth to use available resources (paper, wooden blocks, clay, etc.) along with different modes (rap, legislative theatre or written poems) to think about the redesign of the school where they were studying. There were four modules in this program: (1) storytelling: Youth were asked to tell the whole class about what they liked and disliked about their own community; (2) mapping and building the school: Youth and their co-researchers were given a visual survey, which they conducted on a guided walk, to catalog the layout of their school, then brainstorm what they wanted to build in their school, and report to the whole group about their models; (3) building 3D artifacts: Youth were given papers and architectural blocks to work with their co-researchers to design a 3D model of the item they wanted to build in their

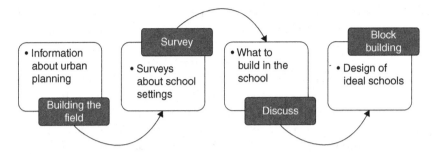

FIGURE 4.1 Spatial Module Sequencing

school (e.g., taco stands or a swimming pool); finally (4) legislative theatre: Youth took part in a role play activity in which they advocated for building their items with the principal or mayor of the city. This chapter reports on the second and third modules: mapping and rebuilding the school.

Within the second module, adult and youth participants were introduced to the concepts of urban design and planning, and participated with the purpose of supporting a re-envisioning of aspects of their school and its grounds. The reason why we were limited to walking the school grounds and mapping the campus as opposed to other locations was largely due to the lack of public transportation in this rural portion of the county. Figure 4.1 outlines the sequenced series of events in the spatial module.

Building the Field

At the beginning of the program, an urban geographer introduced basic concepts of urban design and planning to the group of youth and adult participants. Urban design involves coordinated and self-conscious actions in designing new cities and other human basic needs (e.g., houses, parks, trees, playgrounds and so on) or redesigning existing ones and/or their precincts in response to the needs of their inhabitants (Lang, 2005). In our CS SFL program, the expert in urban planning conducted a short presentation on the overview and key components of urban planning, which was a relatively new concept to both adult and youth participants. The support from an expert helped us to understand more about how to engage in the process of mapping and surveying. In other words, her talk and materials helped us to build the field. The knowledge domain of urban planning includes investigation of social, economic, technological, environmental and political systems that continue to evolve and expand rapidly. The expert provided us with important factors we needed to consider and some basic material considerations such as planning briefs, design briefs, planning frameworks, specific site guidance (topography, zoning, infrastructure and community facilities), city center action plans and so on (Shahreen & Voghera, 2018). As newly ordained urban planners, we found that we needed to take into consideration the area's environment. There are three key areas of environment in this domain: (1) the physical environment such as water or food resources, location of the city or town as well as the area's geologic history; (2) other factors related to social environment, for example, public transportation; finally (3) economic factors (i.e., the socioeconomic levels of residents) (Shahreen & Voghera, 2018).

As the youth participants in this example were middle schoolers, the experts simplified the language and provided concrete information to youth participants. This introduction provided us with knowledge about urban planning, so we could envision the purpose of our upcoming activities.

Conducting Surveys of the School

After introducing these basic concepts of urban planning, our expert asked us to conduct surveys of the school. Namely, before imagining and representing what items could be built and implemented in an idealized recreation of the school, adults and youth participants were asked to conduct a survey of the existing facilities and surroundings. Walking and investigating the school campus helped us to understand and examine the site properly. Armed with generalized maps of the school and its surroundings, we were divided into groups of four or five participants (with adults and youth in each group) and went around the school and took notes. Throughout the activity youth were the experts as they shared with their co-researchers (pre-service teachers, university professors, graduate students and an English for Speakers of Other Languages (ESOL) teacher) their knowledge of the school campus. The discourse among the youth and adults tended to be highly contextualized with the use of deictics (e.g., over there, this building…), gestures (pointing and waving) and concrete descriptions (gray building, community garden).

In this activity, youth were positioned as experts as they had more experience in and around the space of the school. Their lived experience, in other words, was centered and valued. Each group went around and discussed different questions in the survey. This activity helped us to know more about the school setting. Youth also felt more confident about this activity because they had more knowledge about the school than most of the adults did. They supported adults when we had questions. On the other hand, if they did not understand any particular vocabulary items, they felt comfortable asking for clarification. And in the process, information was exchanged. This activity helped us to have a general picture about the students' values in relation to the school grounds; rolled up in the tour of the space were stories about what they appreciated and what they'd change. In addition, through this activity, adult and youth participants created a more holistic view of the school, noting the ways in which windows placement, doors access or out-building location affected perceptions of the school and its attendant spaces. Additionally, the survey experience helped youth participants clarify possible ways in which they might want to re-envision the school.

Discussing the School Campus

After observing and sketching the school, youth and adult researchers discussed different elements the middle schoolers wanted added to the school environment, including more trees, a taco stand and outdoor benches. Others recommended putting in a community garden as they thought it would be a great place for students to gain some ownership over the agriculture of the space.

Surveying the school with maps helped youth participants become more confident in their communication. Without engaging in the spatial modality, students might have needed an expanded set of linguistic resources to achieve the same communicative purpose. For example, Cindy, a young African-American girl, talked about what she observed and what she wanted: "We are going to put the golf course on this side because there is a quite a big place on there." With recourse to the map and feeling comfortable with her co researchers, Cindy felt confident and also excited about showing exactly where she wanted to put her dream golf course. The survey work, in other words, was a chance for the youth to recognize elements that existed in the periphery of their schooled experiences everyday (i.e., a large empty field) and consider how they might be repurposed to better or at least differently service student and community needs. In the same vein, through the embodied and spatial modes of walking, talking and visualizing elements of the school, youth felt excited about sharing their ideas to the adult participants:

> *Adult*: So, what else did you have? You had mini-golf, and I see a lot of other stuff.
> *Youth*: In our field back here (points to top of paper) it's like a big field (sweeps hand in air above paper) and we can add stuff to it if we wanted (swirls hand in air over paper).

This embodied activity supported all participants to interact in highly concrete and context-dependent ways (e.g., youth pointed to the top of the paper and said, "in our field back **here**"). For some of the youth, conversations about what they valued—as manifest in their reshaped school spaces—in a learning environment, felt available for the first time after the mapping exercise. Immersion in spatial and survey activities enhanced students' verbal processing which was complemented through the use of visual artifacts and the use of other semiotic resources such as the survey and map. Mapping the school helped youth and adult participants explore what might be missing from their daily schooled lives. Moreover, a survey helped participants figure out the affordances of the available land—and its constituent elements—in order to collectively reconceptualize the space.

Block Building

Immediately following the walking tours, surveying and mapping, youth were asked to re-construct the school space, differently. Through the use of wooden blocks, youth and adult researchers were positioned as equal partners in building new structures for the school in what was a fairly complex building process. Haptic, verbal and visual modes of interaction intertwined in the meaning-making process as the small groups used the building blocks to build their dream additional resources with use of different sizes and shapes. In this activity, adults and youth used their spatial and perspectival understandings to decide where to put the blocks. Discursively, they used negotiation, concrete descriptors and suggestions in interacting.

Use of building blocks helped the youth and adults lay out the exact position of each item they wanted added to the overall picture of the school grounds. Indeed, as a form of material semiotics, the wooden block pieces were hard and solid in texture, and were physically differentiated by height, width and shape. This range of blocks supported students in visualizing the spatial and scalar dimensions of the school. Wooden blocks gave youth the opportunity to translate their drawing and thoughts on paper into models. With these blocks, youth could build their ideal schools. This process helped them vividly envision layout, and structure; in addition, these models supported youth in articulating their ideal schools to a shared potential audience in the final event of this module.

Presentation of Ideal Schools

A well-structured presentation that includes compelling argument, reasoning and illustration of one's new design that will be pitched to city council and other stakeholders is a highly important part of being an urban planner. Preparing for this process encourages designers to discuss, in particular, the style of report writing, effective argumentation and the use of drawings and three-dimensional materials in an urban design project. For example, Lucia, a shy newcomer bilingual learner from Mexico, presented her final wooden block model with confidence to a large audience as she could demonstrate her spatial, material and visual understandings by using the constellation of blocks and her cumulative knowledge about the design that she gained from her discussions and embodied activities with her partners. Through a co-articulation of verbal, gestural and action resources, Lucia co-constructed meaning with her audience and was recognized by the group as an accomplished presenter. That is, use of the multi-representational resources supported her in co-constructing a social context to create, embody and articulate her thoughts and vision for a new dynamic resource in the school (Gibbons, 2006). The wooden blocks, in this process, became an essential ingredient in the experiential process of learning to scale, situate and assess the newly designed structure, and explain how it would complement existing school resources.

Discussion and Implications

This chapter has shown the various ways in which youth have used materials (i.e., maps and blocks) as semiotic resources in their work, each employment for three different purposes: as resources providing meaning, as communicative tools and as presentational tools.

As for the first purpose, youth used maps as tools to help them provide meaning. Each available mode and material supported youth in generating deep knowledge through relating and constructing meaning in embodied ways that move far beyond more traditional focuses on skills, such as reading or writing, as a way to pass tests in school instruction. The maps provide situated context (i.e., we were here, in this space, and we might put x resource in to make it a place that's different) and with the maps, youth focused more on exploring the positions of each item rather than paying attention to shape, colors or materials of windows, which photos may provide youth. Youth meaning-making was entangled in the materials' meaning potential. Different materials bring different perspectives and different approaches to youth (Frejd, 2018). Therefore, each mode has different affordances and meaning-making potential. This work calls for the use of a multimodal ensemble, where teachers and community educators provide youth with access to multiple meaning-making resources to articulate their ideas. As we discussed earlier, going around the school or neighborhood and discussing its structure with adult participants enabled youth to critically think about the presence and absence of their community's resources (Aitken, 2001). In addition, maps provide representation of youth worldviews and structures of knowledge. Through maps, youth demonstrate how much they know about their schools and what they want to do in order to improve their school structure. The improvement of the school is thus connected to youths' worldview and the process allows youth to reconceptualize their living world.

This chapter also showed that youth use maps and blocks as communicative tools. Blocks were often referred to as "this one" or "that one," in combination with deictic gestures (i.e., pointing at the blocks), instead of adopting the name of the objects. Youth moved the blocks and organized them to represent an ideal school. In the same vein, Jaipal (2010) argues that humans avail themselves of gestures together with their verbal language to reinforce meanings. In our programs, the materials used with communicative modes such as gestures reflect and extend youths' meaning-making potential. Working in the same context with the support from adult researchers makes it possible for youth to collaboratively construct potential meanings and discuss the construction of ideal schools. This process allows youth to generate new knowledge in concert with others in the space.

Youth also use blocks as presentational tools. Instead of using verbal statements (alone) to present ideas about ideal schools, the youth had recourse to blocks to design their own new spaces. This helps an audience visualize and listen to their ideas at the same time. In other words, materials, gestures, movement and words carry the ideational (Ormerod & Ivanic, 2000). Youth used different shapes of blocks as a medium for text production. For examples, Lucia used rectangular blocks to illustrate grade 6, grade 7 and grade 8 buildings. All choices and applications of those blocks are semiotically significant. That significance is socially and culturally shaped, individually constituted and situationally specific.

The activities in this module also demonstrate the interaction between SFL and critical geographic studies. Informed by SFL, a theory of meaning making, maps and blocks are considered tools that help youth to convey and expand their meaning to an audience. The impact of space and place on their identity, and how those concepts make clear the asymmetry of power that marginalizes people of color (Warf, 2004) can be interpreted by seeing what youth desired to build in their school. For example, as in our program, when youth observed the school, they imagined the presence of taco stands which served their favorite food. We asked youth to describe their school (e.g., layout of the windows, colors of buildings or school structure) in order to point out how much they understood the world from spatial perspectives. We gave youth opportunities to examine the way that space is constructed or how it impacts place and identity. As we mentioned earlier, space, a physical location, can be transformed into place (from critical geographic perspective) through investment (Helfenbein, 2006). And we find investment, in our youth community research contexts, comes through relationships constructed with interested adults through multiple semiotic resources, when research questions are carefully targeted at a field (here the schools or neighborhoods of the youth involved) to which youth are well connected. What do we learn, in other words, by walking with youth in the spaces they inhabit, open to their insights about what might be different about their lives, their places, were we to reconstruct them not only with blocks, but with scalable materials as well?

Praxis

Developing Youth Awareness of Surrounding Community

Youth are immersed in a diverse communicational world. Teachers need to provide platforms for youth to activate critical thinking about their neighborhoods and the communities in which they live. Mapping is one tool to promote youth inquiry. Walking around and mapping a school or community allows for spatial orientations and cognitive re-orderings in the reimagination of space. This process also helps youth become more aware of what is still missing in their school. Critical geography studies support youth and adults to practice the questioning of equity of space and place and offer ways to become agents of transformation over time. As Jason Mizell highlighted in Chapter 3, one of our youth participants, Cierra, convinced us to open art and literacy programs at a closed community center because of her vision of what community should be. What could you do to support this approach in your context?

Using Varied Semiotic Resources in Teaching

Providing an intergenerational space where youth can use a range of modes, materials and physical engagement as meaning-making resources and communicative tools is essential in multilingual and multicultural classroom (e.g., giving youth opportunities to use blocks or drawings to articulate their thoughts). Negotiation in choosing materials, colors and shapes of the objects promotes critical media awareness. During the designing process, youth can question their adult co-researchers about the materials, vocabulary items or structure of the school. This helps them build up their knowledge while using the materials at hand. As illustrated in this chapter, youths demonstrate extraordinary skill in making meaning through the affordances of mapping, guided walks and block building. What resources can you use to support your multilingual students in accessing rich disciplinary knowledge in meaningful, multimodal and embodied ways? How would you organize your teaching across these modes?

References

Aitken, S. C. (2001). *Geographies of young people: The morally contested spaces of identity* (Vol. 14). London, UK: Routledge.

Akom, A., Shah, A., & Nakai, A. (2014). Visualizing change: Using technology and participatory research to engage youth in urban planning and health promotion. In H. R. Hall, C. C. Robinson, & A. Kohli (Eds.) *Uprooting urban America: Multidisciplinary perspectives on race, class & gentrification* (pp. 93–106). New York, NY: Peter Lang.

Blundell, D. (2016). *Rethinking children's spaces and places.* New York, NY: Bloomsbury.

Brydon-Miller, M., Kral, M., Maguire, P.,' Noffke, S., & Sabhlok, A. (2011). Jazz and the banyan tree: Roots and riffs on participatory action research. In N. K. Denzin & Y. S. Lincoln (Eds.) *The SAGE handbook on qualitative research* (Vol. 4) (pp. 387–400). Thousand Oaks, CA: SAGE.

Cresswell, T. (2004). *Place: A short introduction.* New York, NY: Blackwell.

Denzin, N. K., & Lincoln, Y. S. (2011). Locating the field. In N. K. Denzin & Y. S. Lincoln (Eds.) *The SAGE handbook on qualitative research* (Vol. 4) (pp. 21–25). Thousand Oaks, CA: SAGE.

Frejd, J. (2018). 'If It Lived Here, It Would Die.' Children's use of materials as semiotic resources in group discussions about evolution. *Journal of Research in Childhood Education, 32*(3), 251–267. doi: 10.1080/02568543.2018.1465497.

Gibbons, P. (2006). *Bridging discourses in the ESL classroom: Students, teachers and researchers.* London and New York: Continuum.

Harman, R. (2018). Transforming normative discourses of schooling: Critical systemic functional linguistics praxis. In R. Harman (Ed.) *Bilingual learners and social equity: Critical approaches to systemic functional linguistics* (pp. 1–21). Cham, CH: Springer International.

Hasan, R. (2011). A timeless journey: On the past and future of present knowledge. In J. Webster (Ed.) *Selected works of Ruqaiya Hasan on applied linguistics* (pp. xiv–xliii). Beijing, CN: Foreign Language Teaching and Research Press.

Helfenbein, R. J. (2006). Space, place, and identity in the teaching of history: Using critical geography to teach teachers in the American south. In A. Segall, E. Heilman, & C. Cherryholmes (Eds.) *Social studies – the next generation: Researching the postmodern* (pp. 111–124). New York, NY: Peter Lang.

Jaipal, K. (2010). Meaning making through multiple modalities in a biology classroom: A multimodal semiotics discourse analysis. *Science Education, 94*(1), 48–72.

Katz, C. (2005). Lost and found: The imagined geographies of American studies. *Prospects, 30,* 17–25.

Lang, J. T. (2005). *Urban design: A typology of procedures and products.* Oxford, UK: Elsevier.

Literat, L. (2013). Participatory mapping with urban youth: The visual elicitation of socio-spatial research data. *Learning, Media and Technology, 38*(2), 198–216.

Nespor, J. (1997). *Tangled up in school: Politics, space, bodies, and signs in the educational process.* Mahwah, NJ: Lawrence Erlbaum.

Ormerod, F., & Ivanic, R. (2000). Texts in practices: Interpreting the physical characteristics of children's project work. In D. Barton, M. Hamilton, & R. Ivanic (Eds.) *Situated literacies: Reading and writing in context* (pp. 91–107). London, UK: Routledge.

Pacheco, D., & Velez, V. N. (2009). Maps, mapmaking, and critical pedagogy: Exploring GIS and maps as a teaching tool for social change. *Seattle Journal for Social Justice, 8*(1), 273–302.

Schleppegrell, M., & Moore, J. (2018). Linguistic tools for supporting emergent critical language awareness in elementary school. In R. Harman (Ed.) *Bilingual learners and social equity: Critical approaches to systemic functional linguistics* (pp. 23–44). Cham, CH: Springer International.

Shahreen, F., & Voghera, A. (May, 2018). Urban planning and design methods for sustainable development. Retrieved April 22, 2019 from https://www.researchgate.net/publication/265922689_Urban_planning_and_design_methods_for_sustainable_development

Soja, E. (1989). *Postmodern geographies: The reassertion of space in critical social theory.* New York, NY: Verso.

Tuan, Y. F. (1979). Space and place: Humanistic perspective. *Progress in Geography, 6,* 211–252.

Warf, B. (2004). Advancing human geography at the commencement du siècle. *The Professional Geographer, 56*(1), 44–52.

PRELUDE TO CHAPTERS 5 AND 6

Movement, Hip Hop and Performance: Integral Components of CS SFL Praxis

Chapter 4 provided readers with an understanding of the affordances of mapping, surveying, photovoice and neighborhood walking for our programs. Chapters 5 and 6 explore how and why play, movement, spoken word and performance are integral components of our work alongside youth and adults who come with imaginative reconceptualizations of what collaborative play means and how it functions. As hooks (1994) articulates about power relationships in education, generally "the person who is most powerful has the privilege of denying their body" (p. 137). To disrupt these dynamics in our work, we use embodied inquiry into our work in a way that puts facilitators, youth and adult co-researchers on an equally vulnerable platform.

As discussed in previous chapters, our CS SFL work with youth privileges community relationship building above all else. However, as often our projects are housed in institutional spaces that can be haunted with oppressive experiences especially for your youth members, we most often come to our collaboration with preconceived notions of teacher/student social identities and school space. To attempt to disrupt these dominant narratives, we have found play a rich resource to position the intergenerational group on a more equal footing. We introduce a play frame through use of improvisation and theater games where performers and spectators interact in spontaneous ways that push them out of the usual institutional frames of references (Partington, 2006).

From the very first day of our programs, we use theater to support a dismantling of institutional walls, even if this desire is somewhat quixotic. We also invite hip hop experts to guide us through workshops and support our amateur play with rhythm, appraisal and movement. Hip hop has a special place in the lives and artistic performances of our youth participants as its history, collaborative practices and improvisation most often convey highly critical and creative challenges to dominant mainstream norms. As Parker (2017) states, "In battle with the oppressive conditions which seek to constrain Black American life, hip hop ideologies are consciously and defiantly constructed against dominant cultural norms and push to create space for the marginalized" (p. 43). Indeed, Alim (2011) noted the highly innovative hip hop practices of youth across the globe whose work moves against institutionally sanctioned norms of creativity. By bringing hip hop into our curriculum, we aim to support such creative remixing of new sounds, visions and performances.

For the past 15 years, Ruth Harman and her colleagues also have incorporated theater as a crucial component of their work with youth and teachers (e.g., Harman & French, 2014; Harman & Varga-Dobai, 2014; Harman & Zhang, 2016). Drawing from the forum theater work of Boal in Brazil, the theatrical components support participants in embodying and reconceptualizing lived experiences in institutional and community contexts. As Harman and Varga-Dobai state,

> Our approach provided student participants with a space in which the learning of new concepts and literacy skills, such as expository writing, occurred within the context of reflective discussions on their lived experience as newly arrived immigrants. Participants used a range of genres in their oral and written discourse (e.g., storytelling, dramatic replay, discussion and newsletter writing) to communicate their emotions and research about immigration issues. In addition, the group became more tightly affiliated through the constant retelling of shared experiences within the classroom, when visitors came to the classroom, and through shared activities that occurred outside of the classroom, such as conference presentations. (p. 13).

In all our CS SFL programs we have found this work to be crucial in supporting our groups in moving toward public articulations of protest and innovative argumentation for social change.

Indeed, Greene (2001) asserted that only through experiential and aesthetic interaction, can we as learners of the world develop a deeper critical awareness of ourselves as embodied civic agents in everyday life. Our performance pedagogy within the CS SFL praxis functions as a dialogic and multidimensional process that provides participants with a space to embody and critically engage with local issues in playful and embodied ways that promote critical awareness (Harman & French, 2004). We encourage educators in and out of school classrooms to also engage in an embodied and playful teaching and learning cycle (TLC) that supports interconnected use of]physical, semiotic and knowledge domains (Siffrinn & Harman, 2019). As Freire (1998) stated, teachers "from the first day of class, must demonstrate to students the importance of imagination for life. Imagination helps curiosity and inventiveness, just as it enhances adventure, without which we cannot create" (p. 51). Instead of hiding our bodies behind opaque cloaks of institutional authority, the cultural, semiotic and material resources bring us collaborative disciplinary and social understandings (Potts & Moran, 2013).

References

Alim, S. H. (2011). Global ill-literacies: Hip hop cultures, youth identities, and the politics of literacy. *Review of Research in Education, 35*, 120–146.

Freire, P. (1998). *Teachers as cultural workers: Letters to those who dare to teach.* (D. Macedo, D. Koike, & A. Oliveira, Trans.). Boulder, CO: Westview Press.

Greene, M. (2001). *Variations on a blue guitar: The Lincoln Center Institute Lectures on aesthetic education.* New York: Teachers College Press.

Harman, R., & Zhang, X. (2015). Performance, performativity and second language identities. *Linguistics and Education, 32*(A), 68–81.

Harman, R., & Dobai-Varga, K. (2012). Critical performative pedagogy: Emergent bilingual learners challenge local immigration issues. *International Journal of Multicultural Education, 14*(2), 1–17.

Harman, R. & French, K. (2004). Critical performative pedagogy: A feasible praxis in teacher education? In J. O'Donnell, M. Pruyn and R. Chavez (Eds.), *Social justice in these times* (pp. 97–116). Greenwich, CT: New Information Press.

hooks, b. (1994). *Teaching to transgress: Education as the practice of freedom.* New York, NY: Routledge.

Parker, M. (2017). *Flippin' the script, joustin' from the mouth: A systemic functional linguistic approach to hip hop discourse.* Unpublished master's thesis, University of Georgia.

Partington, A. (2006). *The linguistics of laughter: A corpus-assisted study of laughter-talk.* London and New York: Routledge.

Potts, D., & Moran, M. J. (2013). Mediating multilingual children's language resources. *Language and Education, 27*(5), 451–468.

Siffrinn, N., & Harman, R. (2019). Toward an embodied systemic functional linguistics. *TESOL Quarterly.* Retrieved December 19, 2019, from https://doi.org/10.1002/tesq.516

5

CS SFL PRAXIS: LANGUAGE PLAY

Mariah Parker and Ruth M. Harman

Poetic and Artistic Language

The use of linguistics in the analysis of language play can be traced back to Aristotle's *Poetics*, which explores how poetic language functions through a combination of everyday language with the use of metaphor, foreign words and lengthened words. In the 20th century, it was linguists such as Roman Jakobson and Jan Mukarovsk in the Prague Linguistic Circle who placed a particular focus on the language of poetics in their work and explored how it functioned differently from other uses (Carter, 1997; Goodman & O'Halloran, 2006). In everyday uses of language, a text generally includes a reference to an external reality; in other words, the referential function is a key ingredient in most communicative acts. In privileging the poetic function in language, on the other hand, Jakobson (1985) sees literary writers as focusing on language itself and not on the referential context.

One key literary concept for the Prague School was the poetic process of defamiliarization. For example, the opening of James Joyce's (1939, p. 1) *Finnegan's Wake* uses old French, contracted wordplay and ellipses to describe Sir Tristan's arrival: "Sir Tristan, violer d'amores, fr'over the short sea, had passencore rearrived from North Armorica." Joyce breaks from the expected referential function of literary prose by using old French (violer d'amores), words that are a lexical mix of French and English (passencore), an ancient Gaulish expression (Armorica) and contractions (fr'over). Because the terms and the way they are combined in Joyce's text are unconventional ways of expressing the story of Tristan's return to Brittany, the Prague School would see readers as necessarily forced to slow down the indexical speed at which they normally read a traditional narrative; slowly the focus needs to settle on the unfamiliar set of syntagmatic (i.e., words that co-occur in the same sentence) and paradigmatic choices (i.e., words that are semantically close and can be substituted one for the other lexical patterns of combining and selecting).

The Prague Circle also saw foregrounding as a key concept in the poetic process. They analyzed how literary writers use linguistic devices such as phonological parallelism (e.g., she sees deep seas), lexical repetition and unusual collocations (i.e., combination of words) that lead to a foregrounding of a pattern of meaning or expression in a text. Taking a YA novel as an example, Spinelli (1990) uses a simple poem to introduce the main character to young adults (p. 2):

Ma-niac, Ma-niac
He's so cool
Ma-niac, Ma-niac
Don't go to school
Runs all night
Runs all right
Ma-niac, Ma-niac
Kissed a bull!

In this short poem, Spinelli (1990) uses rhyme, lexical repetition, theme iteration and phonological parallelism (e.g., "Runs all night," "Runs all right") to express the playful message about the legendary protagonist, Maniac Magee. In other words, he foregrounds certain lexical, grammatical and phonological patterns for poetic effect and textual cohesion.

In contemporary times, linguists have turned their attention to the ways hip hop artists also have foregrounded the poetic functions of language in their rap lyrics and freestyled verses (Parker, 2017). Rappers center cadence, repetition and phonological parallelism in their impressionistic verbal renderings of their experiences, as exemplified in Atlanta rapper J.I.D.'s "151 Rum" (accessible at https://www.youtube.com/watch?v=vtY8pM-H65c). J.I.D. compels listeners to enact movement and other forms of response as he, ostensibly, describes a young man running from gunfire, numbing his pain and ultimately retaliating. But what's more compelling than this story's external reference is its inventive breach of everyday language norms, found in its bounce-inducing and rapid-fire rhythms, rhymes and repetitions.

According to the Prague School, similar to a figure outlined in black against a white background in an expressionist painting, the literary foregrounding of specific patterns and novel expressions in a poetic text is clearly distinct from mainstream uses of language (Jakobson, 1985).

Literary and Everyday Linguistic Play

In contrast to the Prague School's exploration of the difference between literary and non-literary language, research in more recent times has focused on the literariness of language in everyday interactions such as in jokes, puns, advertisements and newspaper headlines (Carter, 1999; Carter & McCarthy, 2004; Cook, 1994; Kramsch & Kramsch, 2000). Carter (2005), for example, explores how a cline of literariness can be explored on a continuum from literary to non-literary uses of language. For Carter, all texts can be analyzed on this cline by the presence or absence of certain linguistic and structural elements. Below is a summary of some of his findings about what constitutes literariness in a stretch of text.

1. A hybrid mix of genres that is not found in more conventional uses of language such as in legal or business discourse.
2. A high degree of interaction among the linguistic levels that leads to a higher level of semantic density than in texts on a lower cline of literariness.
3. Parts of the text are polysemic and can be read on literal or figurative levels.
4. A spatio-temporal displacement of the writer and reader. They rarely inhabit the same space except in performance pieces that are improvised for a live audience.

Carter's highlighting of this interactive play among levels of language and semantic play between metaphorical and literal meanings relates closely to the Prague Circle's concepts of foregrounding and defamiliarization. Carter and McCarthy (2004) and Kramsch and Kramsch (2000) contend that an exploration of this continuum of literariness, from everyday jokes to books of poetry, can be used as a tool in teaching critical language awareness in educational settings. For example, by exploring how everyday language shares similar elements of creativity with "literary texts," students learn to respond to literature with a less rigid distinction between what is "literature" and what is not. In other words, it demystifies and indeed deconstructs the canonical distinction between the "literary" and "non-literary." Secondly, a metalinguistic awareness of how jokes and other daily interactions work through a foregrounding of word play can support students' own literary playfulness and resistance to normative conventions. As Kramsch and Kramsch (2000) state, "the time has come ... to show how crucial this poetic dimension is to language learners, to language teachers, and to the linguistic individuals that we all are" (p. 570).

For Williams (1998) such linguistic play is already part of children's everyday textual practices, especially at early ages, and can be used through explicit scaffolding as the stepping stone to an understanding of language as a pliable resource. In sum, reflecting on language play through an exploration of literariness on a continuum can encourage teachers and students to explore, play and challenge linguistic choices in all its different strata (e.g., phonological, grammatical and semantic).

Critical Linguistics

What occurs often in everyday use of language is that through socialization into normative ways of talking and writing (e.g., generic and register conventions), a discourse community often gets habituated into using "fossilized" and oppressive ways of talking and writing without any critical reflection. That is, "categories encoded in language may become fossilized and unconscious and they may be the products and tools of repressive and inequitable society" (Fowler, 1986, p. 34). The power of linguistic innovation such as defamiliarization, therefore, is that it can be used in everyday contexts to challenge and subvert habituated ways of constructing reality and relationships. In other words, by picking up and using these techniques in everyday contexts, language users can choose to play the game or play with the game for "defamiliarizing techniques are simply an extreme case of techniques of language which are available to all practitioners of language" (Fowler, 1986, p. 37).

A critical linguistic approach is an important one to use in educational settings; it can provide students with an understanding of how language play is a multilayered and intertextual resource used to resist or maintain habitual conventions and expectations of mainstream discourse communities.

Cognitive Poetics and Literary Language

Another important contribution to this discussion about the value of using language play in educational and community settings comes from the combined field of cognitive poetics and linguistic analysis (Semino, 1997, 2005). Cognitive poetics can be defined as a relatively new form of literary criticism that applies the principles of cognitive science to the interpretation of literary texts. Similar to Carter's (1997) concept of a cline of literariness in texts, most scholars in cognitive poetics hold the view that literary texts avail of the same linguistic and cognitive resources as non-literary texts. However, the innovative use of these resources impacts readers in sometimes startlingly creative ways. For instance, Cook (1994) sees literary texts as a key way of challenging and altering existing schemata in readers. The disruption of readers' schemata at higher processing levels is accompanied by unexpected patterns of meaning encountered at the linguistic-structural level. For example, the discourse deviation of a literary text at the structural level (or at the lexico-grammatical level, e.g., Joyce's (1979) *Finnegan's Wake* that continually plays with language at all strata) may disrupt readers' background knowledge about text types or language which may lead to creative expression and thinking.

These studies in cognitive poetics and critical linguistics are important for youth studies. They undermine arguments for mandated simplified curriculum, truncated texts and rote test preparation, which supposedly prepare children to work and succeed in the current global workforce. Instead, these studies show how it is highly complex linguistic work that elicits a change in cognitive understanding.

Creativity and Language Play in CS SFL Praxis

A key element in our CS SFL work with youth is community relationship building through language and physical play. As youth and adults in a school space, we most often come to our project with preconceived notions of teacher/student social identities and school space. To attempt to disrupt these dominant narratives, we have found play to be a rich resource to position the intergenerational group on a more equal footing. In other words, we introduce a play frame through our use of improvisation and theater games that push performers and spectators to interact in spontaneous ways and out of the usual institutional frames of references (Partington, 2006). In a written reflection, one of the pre-service teachers stated the following:

> Yesterday, two things stood out to me as it relates to co-creation of knowledge. The first, was the improv game we played beforehand. In this game, two people with a particular relationship would be talking and then have to switch one person out for another in a different situation but using the same last line. It was so funny. The adults did an excellent job of erasing the barriers between the age lines, and by the last one, the entire audience had figured out how to say "switch" at the funniest moments. The students were able to create the humorous tone as the adults also were. It was so good. (Floria, Reflections 2017)

What Floria appreciated in our use of theater games was the collapse of barriers through the physical and linguistic interactions among the players. By becoming engrossed in the play frame, the participants lost inhibitions about age or other differences, beginning to "erase the age lines."

To engage in this play frame each week of our programs, the group facilitators generate a space where movement, dance and playful verbal exchange can indicate to all participants that we are no longer in a restricted formal space, but instead in an imaginative domain. Theater games involving adults and youth throwing imaginary balls at each other and citing nonsensical words (Bippity Bop; Zip Zap Zop) support a shift into innovative meaning making and embodied relational learning. After one such set of play activities, a graduate student noticed how her youth partner started to convey a much freer use of space and physical movement:

> When Sergio was loosened up after our first two improvisational activities and we went outside, which lent our interactions even more of an informal context, I saw him do a hip-hop dance move to himself, spin, and turn around. It seemed like a dancing version of expressing his freedom, such as when people whistle or hum to themselves when they are happy, but in bodily movements. (Julia, field notes, 2018)

What is clear from Julia's field notes is that Sergio privileges hip hop movement and dance in his free moments. Indeed, not surprisingly, many of our youth members showed high investment and interest in making hip hop dance, rhythm and poetics. To support language play and appreciation for hip hop poetics, we integrate hip hop in our CS SFL programs where youth and adult co-researchers engage in rhythmic and patterned play with sound, movement and verbal resources. By including hip hop as a curriculum module, we encourage our participants to represent their visions, share their insights and convey their contributions through a valued art form that most often centers their lived experiences and plays against normative discourses about race, class and equity (Akom, 2009; Love, 2016). Like other artistic forms of expression, the immersion in hip hop also supports their playing with defamiliarizing and innovative images and language use.

Mariah Parker, first author on this chapter, is a seasoned artist who performs as a rapper and works as a civic leader in our city. A passionate African-American literacy educator, she infuses our participants with an appreciation for an art form that challenges racism and other forms of social issues and supports playful use of multimodal resources such as rhythm, rhyme and movement. In particular, Mariah draws on the tradition of freestyle rap and the cypher to destabilize institutionalized teacher/student relationships and foster a supportive culture of linguistic rule-bending in the classroom (Emdin, 2013). In hip hop, the cypher is a dynamic, interactive and animated space, generally a semi-enclosed circular physical formation, in which rappers trade improvised rhymes whereas onlookers whoop, gesture, groan, snap and otherwise respond with their words and bodies. When "teachers" and "students" participate in the cypher together, they are put on equal footing, both physically, in their egalitarian spatial arrangement, and socially, as all involved are called to make themselves vulnerable to the messiness of verbal improvisation. As well, all have the chance to explore the meaning-making possibilities afforded by cadence, rhyme and metaphor.

For example, in our CS SFL program 2018, Mariah interacted with us in the following way to move us into a creative collaborative meaning making space. After getting participants to throw a ball to each other in a circle while also throwing out an associated set of words, emulating the turn-taking verbal improvisation of the cypher, Mariah said:

MARIAH: So, do you see what happened just there, everyone? Did you see what happened just there?

MALE SPEAKER: We got a ball.

MARIAH: I know. I was just about to end it, and now, we got a better ball. But maybe, we can come back to it at the end, and do it again. But through trying to make rhymes together, something kind of came out that ended up being the theme. So, we kept talking about different things, but then, everyone kept saying, "I don't know." And that sort of became the big idea that was connected through all the rhymes. And so, sometimes, when you start out thinking about the sound of the words, you can end up with a main idea that was not obvious to you in the first place. So, that's why freestyling can be very fun.

Instead of just making the ball and language play an exercise, Mariah supported the group in seeing how spontaneous collaboration around rhythm, movement and rhyme could lead to innovative theme making. Mariah's organic teaching connects to the vision that Alim (2011) and Kelly (2013) promote in terms of supporting creative and critical thinking about language and literacy through the ingenious artistry of hip hop. In her interaction with one group working on a list of words that they will use to make a rap, she highlights how their list making can support creative use of language:

MARIAH: How's it going? You have a long list of words.

FEMALE SPEAKER: We do, but **[inaudible]** they weren't always exact rhymes, but they led on it.

MARIAH: That's perfect. That's how raps get written. People move... because, if you stay with the usual thing, the thing that matches it perfectly, then you run out. *But if you move it, change it a little bit, it can go on forever.* But now, that you have a really long list, you can choose what words will help tell the story you wanted to tell best. So, did you think of a topic yet?

Through a deep understanding of hip hop, Mariah encourages the youth and adult participants to break away from conventional lists of words and associated rhymes and instead to play with the idea of what a rhyme even is. In that way, they can "go on forever" in their creativity.

In her embodied SFL-informed teaching/learning cycle (TLC) (Siffrinn & Harman, 2019), Mariah moves the group from listening to her rapping, to co-construction of raps in a circle with a ball to consideration of rhyme as a resource for textual cohesion in the individual construction of their own poetry.

As discussed in Chapter 2 of this book, the embodied TLC supports the group in engaging physically, emotionally and verbally in creative language play and poetic expression. In the final cycle, Mariah asks each group to perform their rap and gives them feedback.

FEMALE SPEAKER 4: Sometimes, I have a dream. "I have a dream."
FEMALE SPEAKER 3: Helps me win the game.
FEMALE SPEAKER 5: It shall stay the same.
FEMALE SPEAKER 6: Of fame.
FEMALE SPEAKER 4: I'm playing the piano.
FEMALE SPEAKER 3: I play with my hands.
FEMALE SPEAKER 5: [Inaudible] [00:28:15] were together.
FEMALE SPEAKER 3: We can make it better. No matter what the weather.
FEMALE SPEAKER 5: Friendship is love. I wish we had something – but well, friendship is like music; it's infinite.
FEMALE SPEAKER 3: When I meet yah, I say, "What's up?"
FEMALE SPEAKER 5: Friendships come like waves.
FEMALE SPEAKER 3: What do you think?
FEMALE SPEAKER 5: When you think it's the worst, it's the best. Colors don't matter. Twin souls.
GROUP: Friendship
MARIAH: Great. I think you all did a really excellent job of having the feel of a freestyle session, when you pass the words around as you read it out loud. That was awesome. And I think you did a really great job of making the theme come back again and again, even as the rhymes keep changing. So, you said, "Dream," Right? No? Bad. Colors. But then, you talked about dreams, and different things. Even as the rhyme changed, continuing to think about the main theme, you all did very excellently. Let's give them a clap.

Evidenced in Mariah's feedback is the complex meaning making that hip hop freestyle encouraged the group to make, which involved playing at the expression and semantic levels of language at the same time. As discussed in Chapter 2 about the CS SFL praxis, we encourage all participants to avail of all the semiotic, material and physical resources that they feel makes sense in making meaning for their own purposes. In a multilingual exchange below, the participants felt encouraged to use Spanish and English to play out the sound and rhythm across languages.

SPEAKER 4: Ando tocando el piano.
SPEAKER 3: Juego con las manos
SPEAKER 5: were together.
SPEAKER 3: We can make it better. No matter what the weather.
SPEAKER 5: Amistad es amor. I wish we had something – pero bueno. Amistad es como la música; es infinita

In these hip hop and improvisation scenarios, power dynamics shifted as adults and youth attempted to rhyme to a beat or create a humorous counterpoint in the imaginative space. This playful space had an important role in positioning youth and adults on equal footing and in supporting them in making full use of available repertoires in moving toward expression of the genre of freestyling. Some of our participants have developed a keen interest in developing their poetics, using sound studios at our university to record their latest sound.

Discussion

One pre-service teacher involved with the CS SFL commented on the ways her youth co-researcher became more invested in writing about his design of a trampoline for the school, once they had gone through the hip-hop workshops. She stated:

> Yesterday, when I ran the free write activity, PT started to write another rap about his trampoline idea. Not only did he jump into this faster than he did when hip hop was first introduced, but he kept showing me every new line he wrote. I took a picture of his journal and then left to move around the room, and when I came back he said he had written more and held it up so I could take a new picture. He seemed to really be proud of his creation. (Dovia, Personal Reflection, April 2017)

Dovia could see how the module supported PT in becoming more invested and productive in his design thinking and creativity. Mariah's workshop not only validated an artistic style that many youth members loved, but her use of an embodied TLC supported the pre-service teachers and youth in appreciating the complex nature of freestyling and innovative language play. It also supported novice teachers in seeing the value of collaborative linguistic play in learning and teaching. Silvia, another pre-service teacher stated the following:

> Every week I witness how the project we're, working on at Chestnut Middle school allows the participating students to explore multimodal literacies and activities. This way, they are given the opportunity to uncover the things they like doing and what they are interested in. In addition to that, they find themselves in new circumstances, thus they discover new things about themselves and learn who they are. This is exactly what happened this week when we got the task to write a hip-hop piece that would include the words denoting several random objects. None of the team-members coming from the university had any ties with the hip-hop world, so we weren't really confident in what we were doing. I would never embark on such a task on my own, and I don't think I would have

managed to complete it on my own. However, our end product wasn't very bad, and we were proud of our work. (Silvia, Personal Reflection, April 2017)

Importantly, what is clear from this testimony is that the embodied TLC was not only effective for the youth members of our program. Novice teachers were also involved in physically, emotionally and discursively moving through a complex set of repertoires and modes. Our research has shown that this embodied inquiry and language creativity on the part of teachers also supports them in envisioning and designing a multimodal SFL praxis for their own classrooms that encourages creativity and critical awareness among their students (Harman, Siffrinn, Mizell, & Bui, in press).

Praxis

This chapter explored the richness of language play and innovation and why and how it could be incorporated creative and CS SFL practices. Reasons why and ways in which literary play can be used by practitioners are summarized below:

1. Discussion and analysis of the process of foregrounding and defamiliarization in hip hop can support students' understanding of language as a pliable repertoire of choices to be played with for effects and audiences (e.g., Hasan, 1971, 1985; Toolan, 1988).
2. In connection to the point above, a comparative analysis of everyday texts such as jokes and advertisements with texts that are designated as "literary" can help students see "literariness" in their everyday uses of language (e.g., Carter & McCarthy, 2004; Kramsch & Kramsch, 2000).

To conclude, research underlines how a focus on artistic play can have a crucial role in helping students develop an awareness of how patterns of meaning in texts construct point of view, views of reality and texture. It can also highlight the integral relationship of text and context. As Hasan (1971) states about the reading of literature:

Consistency of foregrounding and thematically motivated use of language patterns ensures a reader's sensitivity to even apparently ordinary phenomena in language, which might elsewhere go unnoticed (Hasan, 1971, p. 311)

In addition, use of hip hop supports participants in appreciating the complex nature of the art form and in using its style and performativity for their own purposes and contexts.

Question for you: How would you design a curriculum that supports youth in learning to appreciate and enact the artistic and embodied play in poetry, hip hop and other imaginative genres?

References

Akom, A. (2009). Critical hip hop pedagogy as a form of liberatory praxis. *Equity & Excellence in Education, 42*(1), 52–66. Retrieved March 14, 2019, from https://doi.org/10.1080/10665680802612519

Alim, S. H. (2011). Global ill-literacies: Hip hop cultures, youth identities, and the politics of literacy. *Review of Research in Education, 35*, 120–146.

Aristotle. (1982). *Poetics.* (Trans. James Hutton). New York, NY: Norton & Co.

Carter, R. (2005). Is there a literary language? In S. Goodman & K. O'Halloran (Eds.) *The art of English: Literary creativity* (pp.80–86). New York, NY: Palgrave MacMillan.

Carter, R., & McCarthy, M. (2004). Talking, creating: Interactional language, creativity, and context. *Applied Linguistics, 25*(1), 62–88.

Carter, R. (1997). *Investigating English discourse: Language, literacy and literature.* London, England: Routledge.

Cook, G. (1994). *Discourse approach to literature.* Oxford, UK: Oxford University Press.

Goodman, S. & O'Halloran, K. (Eds.). (2006). *Art of English: literary creativity.* London, England: Open University.

Emdin, C. (2013). The rap cypher, the battle, and reality pedagogy: Developing communication and argumentation in urban science education. In M. L. Hill & E. Petchauer (Eds.) *Schooling hip-hop: Expanding hip-hop based education across the curriculum* (pp. 11–27). New York, NY: Teachers College Press.

Fowler, R. (1986). *Linguistic criticism.* Oxford, UK: Oxford University Press.

Harman, R., Siffrinn, N., Mizell, J., & Bui, K. (in press). Promoting reflection literacy in pre-service language teacher education: Critical SFL praxis with multilingual youth. In L. Altariste & C. Crosby (Eds.), *Second language writing across PK16 contexts: Intersections of teaching, learning, and development.* Ann Arbor, MI: University of Michigan Press.

Hasan, R. (1971). Rime and reason in literature. In S. Chatman (Ed.), *Literary syle: A symposium* (pp. 299–326). London: Oxford University Press.

Hasan, R. (1985). *Linguistics, language, and verbal art.* Deakin University, Victoria: Deakin University Press.

Jakobson, R. (1985). *Verbal art, verbal sign, verbal time.* K. Pomorska & S. Rudy (Eds.) Minneapolis, MN: University of Minnesota Press.

Joyce, J. (1939). *Finnegan's wake excerpt.* Retrieved May 06, 2019, from http://finwake.com/1024chapter1/1024finn1.htm

Kelly, L. L. (2013). Hip-hop literature: The politics, poetics, and power of hip-hop in the English classroom. *English Journal, 102*(5), 51–56.

Kramsch, C., & Kramsch, O. (2000). The avatars of literature in language study. *Modern Language Journal, 84*, 533–573.

Love, B. (2016). Complex personhood of hip hop & the sensibilities of the culture that fosters knowledge of self & self-determination. *Equity & Excellence in Education, 49*(4), 414–427.

Parker, M. (2017). *Flippin' the script, joustin' from the mouth: A systemic functional linguistic approach to hip hop discourse.* Unpublished master's thesis, University of Georgia.

Partington, A. (2006). *The linguistics of laughter: A corpus-assisted study of laughter-talk.* London: Routledge. Doi.org/10.4324/9780203966570.

Route, D. [J.I.D] (2019, May 1). "151 Rum." [Video file]. Retrieved April 14, 2019, from https://www.youtube.com/watch?v=vtY8pM-H65c

Semino, E. (1997). *Language and world creation in poems and other texts.* London, England: Longman.

Semino, E. (2005). What is cognitive poetics? In S. Goodman & K. O'Halloran (Eds.) *The art of English: Literary creativity* (pp.37–44). New York, NY: Palgrave MacMillan.

Siffrinn, N., & Harman, R. (2019). Toward an embodied systemic functional linguistics. *TESOL Quarterly, 53*(4), 909–1193

Spinelli, J. (1990). *Maniac Magee.* New York, NY: Little Brown and Company.

Toolan, M. (1988). *Narrative: A critical linguistic introduction.* London: Routledge.

Williams, G. (1998). Children entering literate worlds: Perspectives from the study of textual practices. In F. Christie & R. Misson (Eds.) *Literacy and schooling* (pp.18–47). New York, NY: Routledge.

6

CS SFL PRAXIS IN MOTION: HOW PERFORMANCE SUPPORTS EMBODIED INQUIRY

Nicole Siffrinn

In recent years, the body has become a central theme in youth studies. Although much of this youth work has been carried out through relational understandings of space and place (e.g., Farrugia, 2014; Hackett, Procter, & Seymour, 2015), there is also a well-established line of scholarship on young people's identities and bodily "norms" (e.g., Frost, 2010; Prince, 2013). Despite this emphasis on the body, however, Coffey and Watson (2015) argued that "[it] often remains implicit or as a site upon which societal inequalities play out, rather than an active force" (p. 185). In other words, when conceived as a passive slate upon which inequities are inscribed, the body's role in the construction of the self is often overlooked (Siffrinn & McGovern, 2019).

General disregard for the body's role in the production of knowledge and meaning is also evidenced in current educational reform. In interviews with 20 experienced science teachers, for example, Zohar and Agmon (2018) found that rote learning often occurred at the expense of hands-on inquiry and experimentation given an increased focus on test preparation. As scholars of movement literacy have shown, youth in industrialized nations have few opportunities to express themselves physically or to engage in recreation that is creative and unstructured (Kentel, 2003; Kentel & Dobson, 2007). In the state of Georgia where much of our work takes place, this lack of activity is compounded by efforts to block recess requirements for school-aged children (Bluestein, 2019) and ongoing testing initiatives that do little more than promote apathy amongst youth (Chagoya & Harman, 2017). As one of our bilingual youth participants described it, the school day often consists of meaningless routines and memorization:

> It's just extensive, [the teachers] have to go through all this material, break it down even further which still doesn't help because they still rush everything into it, and I don't see that helping as much, because we can see that most of the time we're not learning, we're memorizing content for the test, and keep on advancing into that placement. We just memorize, take the test, and then forget everything we learn.

This student's experience is not atypical, as increased accountability measures often mean pacing guides and a standardized curriculum (Au, 2011), both of which limit students' participation in their learning within and beyond the walls of the classroom (Knoester & Au, 2017). Indeed, these narrow practices come especially at a cost for linguistically and culturally diverse students whose ways of knowing, doing and being are markedly different from the practices and ideologies upheld by the school (Flores & Schissel, 2014). With more attention being given to the role of the body in learning, however, the hope is that youths' creative capacity for making meaning can be more regularly exercised in pedagogic practice.

The purpose of this chapter is therefore to explore how physical and semiotic movement in the form of performance support embodied inquiry. As such, the chapter begins with a review of the literature on embodiment before laying out the components of critical performative pedagogy (CPP). Then, drawing on data from a semester-long *Culturally Sustaining Systemic Functional Linguistics (CS SFL)* program, it illustrates how performance enabled youth to co-construct a range of experiences and knowledge to argue for a new addition to their school. The chapter ends with a discussion of the affordances of body work in addition to considering the pedagogical implications for carrying out similar projects.

Embodied Learning

Although the concept of embodiment is not new, there has been a recent push to explore the meaning-making potential of the body in its own right. McDonald (2012), for example, argued that the body's role in the construction of knowledge and meaning has been overshadowed by other modalities and their theorization as "different kinds of 'languages'" (p. 2). Similarly, Bucholtz and Hall (2016) maintained that the body is not simply an effect of language or discourse. Rather, language and the body are inextricably linked, serving as sites of production for the other. With these arguments in mind, educational researchers have begun to show how classroom knowledge is not only developed experientially in the flesh (e.g., Thom and Roth, 2011), but also how meaning is built and expressed in and through the body in relation to an environment of use (e.g., Siffrinn & Harman, 2019). Embodied learning, as such, is defined in this chapter as the ongoing negotiation of physically engaging in contextualized activity while simultaneously seeking to make sense of it in relational and discursive ways.

In line with this definition, Munro (2018) argued that embodied learning hinges on the inseparability of the mind and the body. Indeed, this connection is important, as it situates the body as an active participant in the learning process, not merely supplemental to other mediating tools such as language. In other words, the body has the capacity to activate other sensorimotor systems, allowing for the emergence of a perceptual knowledge of the self and the world (Stolz, 2014). Knowledge construction, as such, is not simply a mental phenomenon but jointly physical and social too. As Nguyen and Larson (2015) explained, embodied learning involves developing spatialized awareness of the body, creating opportunities for reflection and action in experiential ways, and fostering exploration of the body's participation and positioning in the social world. Although there are many different ways of bringing these elements to life, one approach called CPP remains promising in integrating a focus on embodied learning.

Critical Performative Pedagogy

In CPP, the body is seen as an experiential site of learning (Pineau, 2002). Informed by Boal's (1974) Theater of the Oppressed and Freire's (1970) notion of praxis, CPP seeks to challenge social inequities through embodied reflection and action. While drawing on participants' lived experiences to explore how they are connected to larger systems of power, CPP also encourages participants to reimagine and push back against unjust structures (Harman & French, 2004). The body, then, as a meaning-making resource, is "perceived as inscribed and inscribing people's relationships, engagement, and interpretation of multiple ways and histories of being, experiencing, and living, in the world" (Perry & Medina, 2011, p. 63). In other words, CPP recognizes that the construction of knowledge and meaning happens in a particular social, political and historical context where certain ways of knowing, doing and being are privileged over others.

As a part of the CPP process, participants recursively engage in storytelling, theater games, research and performance (Harman & Varga-Dobai, 2012). Although storytelling helps to build trust and community (Winn & Winn, 2016), theater games help to create a participatory contact zone where issues of power and privilege can be addressed and reconfigured (Torre et al., 2008). After issues of social equity have been brought to the surface, participants are then encouraged to engage in collaborative research to propose a solution to a problem relevant to their lives. This research is then used to create a final performance where participants argue on behalf of their proposed solution. Indeed, by engaging in CPP, participants are empowered to "surface leverage points for resistance and change" (Fine, 2008, p. 215) instead of simply accepting the premise that the issues being studied and embodied are inevitable and not subject to alteration. As Pineau (2002) put it, CPP thus involves both "physical action and activism" (p. 53) and can be seen as a way to engage in whole-body sensemaking.

CS SFL Praxis

The CS SFL program described in this chapter took place at a Title I middle school in rural Georgia. Its aim was to explore school and community issues relevant to the youths' lives. Importantly, the program brought together and was co-constructed by youth and pre-service language teachers, having been made possible by a 21st century Community Learning Center Afterschool Program and a school-university partnership. That is, although the program was built on the principles of CS SFL praxis and advanced through a purposefully sequenced set of modalities (e.g., storytelling, photovoice, environmental design and theater), participants were largely responsible for the content explored and the particulars of each week.

The intergenerational group of participants (ranging from 13 to 50 years old) met once a week for two hours from January to May of 2018. Because these meetings took place at the end of the school day, it was important that students were given the time and space to play and socialize in addition to having the freedom to opt out of or suggest alternatives to the day's activities. As such, nearly all of the sessions began with a game that funneled into a pre-determined activity and work session. Although the activities varied widely, because this chapter focuses on the use of CPP within the program, the data discussed in the following sections will be limited to two particular sessions devoted specifically to the use of drama for social change.

Inquiry on the Move

About midway through the CS SFL program, a trained actor who performed in local theaters was invited to work with the youth and pre-service teachers. Indeed, as in this instance, we have found collaboration with the . wider community is critical to this work, as it helps foster meaningful dialogue and validates youths' lived experiences (Burke, Harman, Hadley, & Mizell, 2018). In engaging in the activities described below, the group had to learn to listen to and trust one another in order to enact, reflect upon and reimagine their various experiences. Although the CPP process was altered slightly to respond to the youths' needs and interests, all four components were used as a catalyst for critical exploration of issues the youth were currently facing. In what follows, we describe how theater games, storytelling, research and performance supported embodied inquiry and social change within their school community.

Theater Games

To begin the first session on CPP, youth and pre-service teachers warmed up by playing a game that involved a conflict. As explained by the facilitator of the game:

FACILITATOR [SPEAKING TO EVERYONE]: We're going to have two people up here, and they're going to have a conflict, so one person wants something, and the other person wants something completely different.
[FACILITATOR ASKS FOR TWO VOLUNTEERS.]
FACILITATOR [SPEAKING TO VOLUNTEER 1]: So, you do not want to shake his hand. You do not want to do it.
VOLUNTEER 1: I can do that.
FACILITATOR [SPEAKING TO VOLUNTEER 2]: You really want to shake her hand, so you're going to try everything you have to get her to shake your hand. The first time we do this, there's going to be no speaking. It's just with your body, alright?
FACILITATOR [SPEAKING TO EVERYONE]: What [the rest of us are] going to do is we're going to watch and see what he is doing, and can you think of a way that maybe he can succeed if he tried something different.

As the game began, the two volunteers worked to achieve their goal. Because talking was not allowed at this juncture, they had to come up with creative ways to get the other to acquiesce by contorting their bodies and gesturing. Indeed, although this short scene provoked laughter from the rest of the group, it also demanded that the body be seen as a form of expression. As Haft (2013) wrote, "the body speaks even when the mouth is silent" (p. 141), as it encodes and is encoded with social and cultural information that must be negotiated in a shared space of action.

Importantly, when talking was introduced into the game, the body's role in the meaning-making process was not diminished. Although the volunteers could be heard asking questions and trying to bribe the other to give in to their request, the body, working in tandem with language, was still actively mediating the experience (Cheville, 2006), as were the social and cultural understandings of what was appropriate or not to do given the gendered dynamic.

Also important, however, was the debriefing that took place after the game, as it encouraged the youth and pre-service teachers to reflect on what worked or did not work and why.

FACILITATOR: What strategies did he try?
YOUTH 1: He tried money. He asked what she wanted.
YOUTH 2: He said, can I be your friend?
FACILITATOR: He asked to be her friend.
YOUTH 3: He gave compliments.
FACILITATOR: He gave compliments. He did succeed after the scene was over. Who has a different idea of what he could try?

Although lighthearted and fun, this simple reflective act along with the game itself prepared participants for the more intensive and meaningful work they would engage in, in relation to conflicts they personally experienced. As Thambu and Balakrishnan (2014) explained, such games provide a means for not only generating ideas but also for increasing participants' ability to explore and respond to real issues they are facing.

Storytelling and Improvisation

In the next phase of the performative process, the facilitator used the handshake game to segue into forum theater. Created by Boal (1998), forum theater provides a means for enacting and reenacting an oppressive situation by allowing audience members to partake in altering the initial outcome. As the facilitator explained to the group:

> We use forum theater to kind of practice for real-life situations where we really want to achieve something or get something or do something, but the other person or institution or school or group is not letting us do what we want to be able to do.

Thus, similar to the handshake game, participants had to improvise and strategize to try to resolve the conflict being performed.

Prior to engaging in forum theater, however, participants were asked to recall and share a time in which they experienced some difficulty getting what they wanted.

FACILITATOR: I want you to talk with the people you're sitting with for a couple minutes, and try to think of a time that you really wanted to be able to have, or do, or get something, maybe in this middle school or maybe at home in the real world, and you just weren't able to do it because of a group or another person. Does everybody understand what I want you to do....so we're going to...think about a conflict that you've had.

Once given time to talk amongst themselves, the facilitator asked for volunteers to share their stories.

YOUTH 1: The teachers won't let us go to the bathroom first period, fourth period or...

FACILITATOR: Okay, so the teachers won't let you go to the bathroom unless...

YOUTH 2: Other times during the day.

FACILITATOR: Oh, my goodness.

YOUTH 1: Some teachers don't...

FACILITATOR: Okay, and do you know why?

YOUTH 3: Because they think we be running.

YOUTH 2: Some girls taking phones in the bathroom and they...

YOUTH 1: Yeah. It's like the sixth stall...

YOUTH 3: And they need lots of fixing because they be busted up and that's nasty.

YOUTH 2: And some boys in the bathroom, they be fighting.

As these issues were brought to the forefront, the facilitator informed everyone that they were going to have an opportunity to play out these scenes and try to solve them. Working with the bathroom scene first, the facilitator asked for a few more details.

FACILITATOR: I think we need to know a little bit more about it. So, what you want, what the hero wants is...can you tell me like in one sentence?

YOUTH 1: I want you to stop drawing on the stalls and stop playing...and for the janitors like to clean up all the bad things really nice.

FACILITATOR: Oh, so it's not, you don't want to be able to use the bathroom at any time. You want people not to abuse the bathroom.

YOUTH 1: Yeah.

ADULT: Yeah or you can't use the bathroom because there's always stuff going on in the bathroom.

YOUTH 1: Yeah.

YOUTH 2: No. They can't use the bathroom every other period. That was initially the problem.

FACILITATOR: Well, tell me what you think about this. If this is not like the same scenario you're describing, just tell me so I understand. What if we had a teacher during one of the periods that you cannot go to the bathroom. So, what this teacher...just like she [pointing at volunteer from previous game] didn't want to shake hands, this teacher is going to say like "No. You cannot go to the bathroom," and we have a student that's going to try to convince this teacher that, even though it's the wrong period, you should be able to go to the bathroom. Is this the situation? Does that sound correct?

Once everyone was in agreement, the facilitator took volunteers to act out the scene. Initially, one youth played the role of the teacher and another youth played the role of the student.

STUDENT: Can I go to the bathroom?
TEACHER: No.
STUDENT: Why?
TEACHER: Because I said so.
STUDENT: Why?
TEACHER: Because I said so.
STUDENT: I got to go...really bad!
TEACHER: Okay. You can wait.
STUDENT: [does a dance]
TEACHER: You can wait until the next period.
STUDENT: But I can't wait.
TEACHER: What do you mean you can't wait?
STUDENT: I can't wait.
TEACHER: Yes, you can.
STUDENT: Why?
TEACHER: Because you're a middle-schooler.
STUDENT: Why?
TEACHER: Therefore, due to your age, you can hold it until it's time.

Once the scene was over, the facilitator asked everyone to reflect on how it unfolded in addition to asking them to consider other strategies for getting what they wanted. These ideas, which included annoying and begging the teacher as well trying to "convince her with science" were reenacted as new volunteers came into the scene. In the end, everyone agreed that arguing to go to the bathroom with scientific evidence would work in a real-life scenario, meaning that they felt they found a solution to their problem. Indeed, the power of forum theater is that it encourages intervention and helps participants begin to see how they might be able to apply similar strategies in real-world environments (Louis, 2005).

In a similar CS SFL program that Ruth directed at the same school several years before (e.g., Harman & Smagorinsky, 2014; Harman & Varga-Dobai, 2012), the CPP process supported 11 Latine girls and their teachers in addressing the serious issues of abrupt deportation and job discrimination due to immigration status. Similar to our CS SFL work in 2018, they focused on physical play, theater and multimodal integration of strong arguments and performance. The girls prepared a performance script that focused on the terrifying moment when police officers knock on the front door of their mobile home early in the morning when a young child may open the door and let them in. The script included the following dialogue:

CLARITA: ¿Alguien quiere más tamales?
CHILDREN: ¡Yo! ¡Yo! ¡Yo! Aqui tienen.
EVA: ¡¡Mamá!! Alguien está tocando la puerta. (*Large knocking on door. Two police officers looking angry.*)
TAMARA: I will get it. Don't worry. (*large knocking*)
POLICE: You need to open up!! (*Tamara opens the door*)
TAMARA: What do you want?
POLICE: Young girl, move over. We are in a hurry. I betcha have some illegal activities going on in here. Let me pass.
MAMA: We have no choice. We need to let them in.
TAMARA: Stop! I am sorry, officers, but do you have a search warrant? (*looking annoyed*)
POLICE: Well, no, okay, but that doesn't stop us. (*Goes to push by her*)
TAMARA: You do not have the right to come in here without a search warrant!! (*Police officers leave*)

In this CPP process, the middle school girls chose to focus on police and migration harassment. In creating and performing the scene above, they used their lived stories, fears and physical action to challenge the bullying practices of local authorities. Similar to our work with youth in the 2018 program, the girls felt a strong sense of solidarity and strength through exploration of their lived emotions and their research on civil rights of all residents in the United States. The bathroom issue described in 2018, for example, allowed the youth to embody and express their concerns in ways they had not previously been able to do due to the institutional discourses they were entrenched in. As one of the youth participants stated after engaging in forum theater, "I learned that we have opinions too."

Research and Dissemination

During the next phase of the critical performative process in 2018, participants broke into groups based on their interests and concerns. Drawing on the content that came up during forum theater, they selected an issue to focus on and began working on a solution that they would then present in argumentative form to the school principal. One of the groups decided to argue on behalf of a fence and a marquee, the former to keep litter off of the school grounds and the latter to highlight student achievements and make school announcements more visible. This research process included locating information about the costs and benefits of adding this structure and resource to the school. It also included constructing an argument out of that information and preparing to perform it in a modality of the youths' choice, which in this case was a rap.

Indeed, for Andre, this choice was important, as it was part of his identity, his story and his repertoire of expression, creating what DeJaynes (2015) referred to as a "textured [site] of inquiry" (p. 186). That is, by constructing an argument in his preferred modality, Andre necessarily wove his personal experience with that of his group members, enabling them to build community and validate their shared vision for a new school structure and resource. It also enabled him to remix a school-sanctioned genre through movement, rhythm and spoken verse. As Turner, Hayes, and Way (2013) illustrated in a similar participatory study, hip hop provided a means for the youth to synthesize the information gathered from their research and integrate it into a socially and culturally relevant understanding of the issues they were facing.

In addition to the rap, the final performance, which was done in front of the school principal, included a multimedia presentation that contained visual evidence as to why the fence and marquee were needed. The principal, in acknowledging their argument, said that she was "definitely going to work on" getting a marquee for the upcoming school year, a statement that was met with applause from the youth. She also said that she was going to "get some names [and] representatives" so that the youth could be part of the planning process for not just the marquee but some of the other resources that were argued for such as new furniture to make the library a more inviting space. This invitation to participate in future decision-making at the school is integral to participatory work with youth, as it opens up a space wherein youth experiences and knowledge have the potential to be heard and valued in addition to being used to inform improvements at the school (Bertrand, 2018). What is more, this validation from the principal in addition to the CPP process as a whole, enabled youth members to begin to see how their bodily, emotional and intellectual investment in the project supported them in reaching a larger audience and in developing a collective that included adults and youth from various local communities. Without the physical play and theater role playing, however, this program would have left the lived insights and strong emotions at the door of the classroom, the usual state of affairs in our high-stakes testing environments.

Discussion

Although all modes are "significant for meaning and communication" (Jewitt and Kress, 2003, p. 2), our work with teachers and youth in this era of accountability has shown us that not all modes are given equal weight in classroom practice. The body, for example, is often stifled as a meaning-making resource, which means that ownership over a literacy, such as hip hop, is unlikely in that space. In using CPP to support embodied inquiry, however, the CS SFL program and its participants challenged institutional discourses about learning and representation in addition to promoting social change within their school community. In Andre's case, the insights gleaned from improvised scenes and interactions were embodied in practice through a rap whereas for others this engagement resulted in a scripted performance, both of which were met with a positive response from the school principal. Indeed, an arts-based process such as CPP not only validates youths' ways of knowing and being, it also supports them in moving beyond mere exploration of their lived experiences to taking action in relevant contexts (O'Connor, 2009).

As the youths' experiences were collaboratively reconstructed, they were also faced with responding to one another by taking on and considering the power relations inherent in different social positions. When one of the youth participants played the role of a teacher denying a student use of the bathroom, for example, she reconfigured her own experience and spoke back to the dominant school order in both a physical and verbal way. As Medina and Campano (2006) explained, CPP provides an "(inter)active context wherein participants can comprehend and stretch the limits of their day-to-day realities through the embodiment of critical reflection and both rehearsed and improvised action" (p. 333). Indeed, this reflective stance, coupled with the embodied and discursive practices within the CPP framework, offered the youth in our CS SFL program a way to negotiate the power-laden discourses they encounter on a daily basis.

Embodying their lived experiences was also critical for the generation of new knowledge. As recent research has shown, using the body as a form of expression can greatly aid conceptual understanding and creative meaning-making (Hendrix, Eick, & Shannon, 2012). During the improvised components of the CPP process, for example, the youth had to draw on all available linguistic and cultural resources to interact with their peers. It was in these moments that new possibilities and transformations became possible or, at the very least, that a space was opened up for "innovative avenues of creative production" (Schmidt & Beucher, 2018, p. 120). There is thus a performative potential in embodying, exploring and reimagining the social issues youth are facing.

Conclusion and Implications

As was illustrated throughout this chapter, CPP provides a way of engaging youth in embodied inquiry that challenges them to take action against inequities in their local environments. It is important to note, however, that building a community of trust is a key first step to this work, especially given the highly personal nature of the issues under exploration. Educators interested in using CPP to enact social change thus might begin with a series of theater games that allow youth to interact with one another in unexpected and humorous ways before delving into more serious topics. Even when moving into forum theater, participants can be encouraged to exaggerate their lived experiences, as doing so may open up a space for different sociopolitical connections to be made (Dwyer, 2004). The point is that the CPP process needs to be purposefully scaffolded so that participants can explore the realities of their daily lives through both embodied reflection and action.

As Shirley Brice Heath (2015) reminds us, embodied engagement in learning is a key element in fostering youth literacy.

> We shape thought in our minds and can gesture, sketch, draw, and model with our hands what we are thinking often before we can express ideas verbally. We can better articulate our thoughts when our nonverbal interior mental work has clarified and censored what we might then go on to express through the use of structured symbol systems, such as those of sign language, speech, or writing. (p. 401)

Indeed, her research in neuroscience has shown that embodiment (i.e., use of the whole or parts of the body in working around and with visual, verbal and action texts) plays a pivotal role in the cognitive and language development of children. The hand, even, is a haptic resource that supports cognitive development that cannot be replaced by digital (i.e., finger) use of computers and screen viewing. Sadly, in our current public schools, especially those that serve low socioeconomic student populations, top down managerial discourses stifle critical discussion and rich experiential learning in classrooms and promote reductive literacy practices that reduce learning to a string of facts to be regurgitated.

Praxis

The objective of our work is to support use of an array of modalities, artistic expressions and inquiry modes so that our participants engage in embodied practices that support their cognitive development, expanded semiotic resources and community solidarity. The ever-present digital screen in classrooms of a lot of middle schools is replaced in our work by art materials, clay, blocks, scales and balls. In performance modules, minoritized youth feel that their insights and experiences are acknowledged and celebrated, often for the first time. As one of our bilingual youth members stated:

> I felt very nervous on the night of the performance, but a friend came on stage with me and helped translate for me as I was speaking in Spanish. I tried to be strong and I followed my father's advice who said not to look at the audience but just to look at a point on the wall. I felt good because the people were understanding how difficult the trip to the United States was and also having to learn all in English (into new life). When they started

clapping, I felt all my hard work I did to learn the story and also to do well in school was worth it. (Harman, Johnson, & Chagoya, 2016, p. 217)

In using CPP, then, we hope to provide youth with a means to explore their daily realities through physical movement and sensory activities to promote the generation of new knowledge for their own social purposes. Here are some questions for you to discuss with your colleagues, students or youth co-researchers:

1. How would you introduce theater and movement into your classroom or community context?
2. What strengths and challenges do you think you would see in doing this work?

References

Au, W. (2011). Teaching under the new Taylorism: High-stakes testing and the standardization of 21st century curriculum. *Journal of Curriculum Studies*, *43*, 25–45.

Bertrand, M. (2018). Youth participatory action research and possibilities for students of color in educational leadership. *Educational Administration Quarterly*, *54*(3), 366–395.

Bluestein, G. (2019, May 10). Update: Georgia governor vetoes mandatory recess, school safety bills. *Atlanta Journal Constitution*. Retrieved July 26 2019, from https://www.ajc.com/blog/politics/veto-day-georgia-governor-set-make-final-decision-key-bills/GzVQoZ48zVUdxuHarMEGHJ/

Boal, A. (1974). *Theatre of the oppressed* (C. McBride & M. L. McBride, Trans.). London, UK: Pluto.

Boal, A. (1998). *Legislative theatre: Using performance to make politics* (A. Jackson, Trans.). London, UK: Routledge.

Bucholtz, M., & Hall, K. (2016). Embodied sociolinguistics. In N. Coupland (Ed.) *Sociolinguistics: Theoretical debates* (pp. 173–198). Cambridge, UK: Cambridge University Press.

Burke, K. J., Harman, R., Hadley, H. L., & Mizell, J. D. (2018). 'I could not believe that would happen': Challenges and opportunities in a critical, project-based clinical experience. *New Educator*, *14*(3), 212–230.

Chagoya, E. E., & Harman, R. (2017). In lockdown: Where is the joy of our youth? *Journal of Language and Literacy Education*, 1–10. Retrieved January 4 2018, from http://jolle.coe.uga.edu/wp-content/uploads/2017/04/chagoya_harman.pdf

Cheville, J. (2006). The bias of materiality in sociocultural research: Reconceiving embodiment. *Mind, Culture, and Activity*, *13*(1), 25–37.

Coffey, J., & Watson, J. (2015). Bodies: Corporeality and embodiment in childhood and youth studies. In J. Wyn & H. Cahill (Eds.) *Handbook of children and youth studies* (pp. 185–200). Singapore, SG: Springer.

DeJaynes, T. (2015). 'Where I'm From' and belonging: A multimodal, cosmopolitan perspective on arts and inquiry. *E-Learning and Digital Media*, *12*(2), 183–198.

Dwyer, P. (2004). Making bodies talk in forum theatre. *Research in Drama Education*, *9*(2), 199–210.

Farrugia, D. (2014). Space and place in studies of childhood and youth. In J. Wyn & H. Cahill (Eds.) *Handbook of children and youth studies* (pp. 1–14). Singapore, SG: Springer.

Fine, M. (2008). An epilogue, of sorts. In J. Cammarota & M. Fine (Eds.) *Revolutionizing education: Youth participatory action research in motion* (pp. 213–234). New York, NY: Routledge.

Flores, N., & Schissel, J. L. (2014). Dynamic bilingualism as the norm: Envisioning a heteroglossic approach to standards-based reform. *TESOL Quarterly, 48*(3), 454–479.

Freire, P. (1970). *Pedagogy of the oppressed* (M. Bergman, Trans.). New York, NY: Herder and Herder.

Frost, L. (2010). Doing bodies differently? Gender, youth, appearance and damage. *Journal of Youth Studies, 6*(1), 53–70.

Hackett, A., Procter, L., & Seymour, J. (2015). *Children's spatialities: Embodiment, emotion and agency.* London, UK: Palgrave Macmillan.

Haft, N. (2013). Jewish gestures. In M. Katz (Ed.) *Moving ideas: Multimodality and embodied learning in communities and schools* (pp. 139–156). New York, NY: Peter Lang.

Harman, R., & French, K. (2004). Critical performative pedagogy: A feasible praxis in teacher education? In J. O'Donnell, M. Pruyn, & R. Chavez (Eds.) *Social justice in these times* (pp. 97–116). Greenwich, CT: New Information Press.

Harman, R., & Smagorinsky, P. (2014). A critical performative process: Supporting the second language literacies and voices of emergent bilingual learners. *Youth Theater Journal, 28*(2), 147–164.

Harman, R., & Varga-Dobai, K. (2012). Critical performative pedagogy: Emergent bilingual learners challenge local immigration issues. *International Journal of Multicultural Education, 14*(2), 1–17.

Heath, S. B. (2015). Creativity and the work of art and science: A cognitive neuroscience perspective. In M. Fleming, L. Bresler, & J. O'Toole (Eds.) *The routledge international handbook of the arts and education* (pp. 398–409). New York, NY: Routledge.

Hendrix, R., Eick, C., & Shannon, D. (2012). The integration of creative drama in an inquiry-based elementary program: The effect on student attitude and conceptual learning. *Journal of Science Teacher Education, 23*, 823–846.

Jewitt, C., & Kress, G. (Eds.). (2003). *Multimodal literacy.* New York, NY: Peter Lang.

Kentel, J. A. (2003). Movement, the lost literacy: What Kenyan children can teach us about active play. *Physical & Health Education Journal, 69*(1), 12–17.

Kentel, J. A., & Dobson, T. M. (2007). Beyond myopic visions of education: Revisiting movement literacy. *Physical Education and Sport Pedagogy, 12*(2), 145–162.

Knoester, M, & Au, W. (2017). Standardized testing and school segregation: Like tinder for fire? *Race Ethnicity and Education, 20*(1), 1–14.

Louis, R. (2005). Performing English, performing bodies: A case for critical performative language pedagogy. *Text and Performance Quarterly, 25*(4), 334–353.

McDonald, E. (2012). Embodiment and meaning: Moving beyond linguistic imperialism in social semiotics. *Social Semiotics, 23*(3), 1–17.

Medina, C. L., & Campano, G. (2006). Performing identities through drama and teatro practices in multilingual classrooms. *Language Arts, 84*(4), 332–341.

Munro, M. (2018). Principles for embodied learning approaches. *South African Theatre Journal, 31*(1), 5–14.

Nguyen, D. J., & Larson, J. B. (2015). Don't forget about the body: Exploring the possibilities of embodied pedagogy. *Innovative Higher Education, 40*(4), 331–344.

O'Connor, P. (2009). Unnoticed miracles. *Research in Drama Education: The Journal of Applied Theatre and Performance, 14*, 583–597.

Perry, M., & Medina, C. (2011). Embodiment and performance in pedagogy research: Investigating the possibility of the body in curriculum experience. *Journal of Curriculum Theorizing, 27*(3), 62–75.

Pineau, E. L. (2002). Critical performative pedagogy. In N. Stucky & C. Wimmer (Eds.) *Teaching performance studies* (pp. 41–55). Carbondale & Edwardsville, IL: Southern Illinois University Press.

Prince, D. (2013). What about place? Considering the role of physical environment on youth imagining of future possible selves. *Journal of Youth Studies, 17*(6), 697–716.

Schmidt, K. M., & Beucher, B. (2018). Embodied literacies and the art of meaning making. *Pedagogies: An International Journal, 13*(2), 119–132.

Siffrinn, N. E., & Harman, R. (2019). Toward an embodied SFL pedagogy. *TESOL Quarterly, 53*(4), 1162–1173.

Siffrinn, N. E., & McGovern, K. R. (2019). Expanding youth participatory action research: A Foucauldian take on youth identities. *International Multilingual Research Journal, 13*(3), 168–180.

Stolz, S. A. (2014). Embodied learning. *Educational Philosophy and Theory, 47*(5), 474–487.

Thambu, N., & Balakrishnan, V. (2014). Forum theatre as a moral education pedagogy. *ATIKAN: Jurnal Kajian Pendidikan, 4*(1), 1–12.

Thom, J. S., & Roth, W. (2011). Radical embodiment and semiotics: Toward a theory of mathematics in the flesh. *Educational Studies in Mathematics, 77*(2-3), 267–284.

Torre, M. E., & Fine, M. with Alexander, N. B., Amir, B., Blanding, Y., Genao, E.,… Marboe, E., Salah, T., & Urdang, K. (2008). Participatory action research in the contact zone. In J. Cammarota & M. Fine (Eds.) *Revolutionizing education: Youth participatory action research in motion* (pp. 23–44). New York, NY: Routledge.

Turner, K. C. N., Hayes, N. V., & Way, K. (2013). Critical multimodal hip hop production: A social justice approach to African American language and literacy practices. *Equity & Excellence in Education, 46*(3), 342–354.

Winn, L. T., & Winn, M. T. (2016). 'We want this to be owned by you': The promise and perils of youth participatory action research. In S. Greene, K. J. Burke, & M. K. McKenna (Eds.) *Youth voices, public spaces, and civic engagement* (pp. 111–130). New York, NY: Routledge.

Zohar, A., & Agmon, V. A. (2018). Raising test scores vs. teaching higher order thinking (HOT): Senior science teachers' views on how several concurrent policies affect classroom practices. *Research in Science & Technological Education, 36*(2), 243–260.

PRELUDE TO CHAPTERS 7 AND 8

Youth Refusal and CS SFL Failures

Prior chapters have introduced you to the theories and praxis of CS SFL that support our work with youth. Chapter 3 featured the testimonios of three youth members invested in shifting the dynamics of race and place in their everyday lives. Chapters 4, 5 and 6 explored how mapping, surveying, movement and other modalities provide youth and adult participants with resources to build alternative designs that challenge the status quo in their schools or neighborhoods. As Derr, Chawla, and Mintzer (2018) state, "place-based participation makes sense because young people want opportunities to shape where they live" (p. 11).

Chapters 7 and 8 turn to a different but highly important focus in our work. The innovative and creative refusals of our youth participants to engage in what we described in Chapter 2 as our purposively sequenced set of multimodal activities that build toward a final performance in front of powerful stakeholders. Instead, some participants choose to move toward alternative art and civic meaning-making in our programs, creating ingenious designs that we adults would never have been able to imagine or construct. These creative refusals and transformations teach us to be loose in holding on to *our* curriculum, to our set of modules and to be open to the wisdom of our participants. The refusals, often, also indicate failure on our part to truly be with our participants, listening and putting their needs and goals at full center.

In Chapter 7, we think about the possibilities opened up through relationship building and ready access to visual and spoken media. We also include discussion of the limitations of our work, always co-present in any youth initiatives we implement. We examine the experience of Heidi Hadley, a graduate student, as she details her experiences with three middle school girls of color as they endure, and resist, our CS SFL community-arts-based curriculum. In the process of resisting the structure of the course, however, the girls—with Heidi as a guide—find their way through multiple media, to a powerful critique of the racist/sexist implications of a culture that provides them precious little space to conduct guided inquiry into literacy activities that might alter their sense of possibility in the world.

Chapter 8 focuses on the CS SFL programs and design in general. We suggest to our readers that too often work in youth pedagogies, and we include our work in this category, glosses over the difficult, uncertain, emotionally draining and failure-intensive reality that comes as a natural part of any community-based work, but particularly such work with youth. Drawing on Diaz-Strong, Luna-Duarte, Gomez, and Meiners' (2014) acknowledgement that "shame, circulating within families and institutions...works to maintain social and institutional silences" (p. 15), we want to dig into the silences in research around refusal and failure in transformative pedagogies noting that when we "story over" (San Pedro, 2017, p. 101) the difficulties of the work—for researchers, for youth, for communities—in search of 'success' or, rather, a research narrative that fits the form of intervention to transformational change, we do an active disservice not only to our colleagues endeavoring to take up the work alongside us, but also of course, to the communities with which we hope to (continue to) work.

References

Derr, V., Chawla, L., & Mintzer, M. (2018). *Placemaking with children and youth: Participatory practices for planning sustainable communities*. New York, NY: New Village Press.

Diaz-Strong, D., Luna-Duarte, M., Gomez, C., & Meiners, E. R. (2014). Too close to the work/there is nothing right now. In D. Paris & M. T. Winn (Eds.) *Humanizing research: Decolonizing qualitative inquiry with youth and communities* (pp. 3–20). Thousand Oaks, CA: SAGE.

San Pedro, T. J. (2017). 'This stuff interests me': Re-centering indigenous paradigms in colonizing schooling spaces. In D. Paris & H. S. Alim (Eds.) *Culturally sustaining pedagogies: Teaching and learning for justice in a changing world* (pp. 99–116). New York, NY: Teachers College Press.

7

CS SFL PRAXIS IN VISUAL AND DIGITAL DESIGN: NARRATIVES OF RESISTANCE AND CREATION

Heidi L. Hadley and Kevin J. Burke

In the summer of 2016 Ruth and Kevin, the primary designers of the *Culturally Sustaining Systemic Functional Linguistics (CS SFL)* summer programs, implemented a curriculum rooted in multiliteracies and youth inquiry. They established the program in the context of a school/university partnership that led to vibrant research and teaching collaborations among university, school and community educators (Kittleson, Dresden, & Wenner, 2013). Specifically, Ruth and Kevin created a graduate course to introduce doctoral and master's students to principles of Youth Participatory Action Research (YPAR) while concurrently running an arts-based inquiry program for middle school youth from the local school district. Their program, in turn, took place in an all-day four-week summer "un-schooling" experience for about 100 local K-8 children run jointly by the school district and the College of Education. In other words, we were just one part of a pretty expansive four-week experience for the kids that we all hoped would move away from a traditional school experience heavy on standardization and the policing of Black and Brown bodies.

Heidi Hadley took part in this inaugural course, as did two of the girls featured in the narratives below. The second version of the course in the summer of 2017, which Heidi also attended and describes here, was relocated to an elementary school in the district. The activities related to the work were adapted to the new location and group—some were kept the same and others shifted based on the previous year's experiences with particular attention paid to developing relationships between adult and youth co-researchers—but the main framework for the class remained the same. In summer 2017, we spent three hours a day, four days a week, for four weeks, partnering middle school and graduate students with the aim that they might co-construct an experience in YPAR using multiple affordances of art. One day a week we all took buses to the state art museum and engaged in experiential activities that linked our community discussions from the elementary school to public art and its uses.

These were the modest goals of the course: The degree to which we succeeded in providing a space for youth and adults to discuss community change through art varied immensely. As we discuss later in this chapter, what successes might have occurred are ones that we might argue are only tangentially related to the—formal, at least—curriculum of the course. We have come to realize that we need more sophisticated ways for thinking about how a curriculum can fall under its own weight, only to be raised up by the relationships developed in the process of resisting a prescribed course of action. Similarly, Heath (1983) found that youth created optimal work when immersed in autonomously running a community arts program. In some ways this is the stuff of youth transformation and youth voice, although it requires a rejiggering of the ways in which we consider failure in research and practice.

It's vital to note, as you read, that one of the major shifts from the first year of the course into the second year elucidated here, had to do with empowering the graduate student/adult co-researchers to mushfake the curriculum with the kids. Mushfaking, for Gee (1989) is a form of discourse that takes account of a "partial acquisition" of a discourse "coupled with meta-knowledge and strategies to 'make-do'" (p. 13). In other words, the relationship building and the youth as center of this relationship prevailed over any macro-course structure. Instead, the idea for our purposes, and we think it is vital to lay this out for readers, is that no one was expert in the research work of the course. We were all mushfaking, depending on the improvisational moves handed to us by our partners. In following on culturally sustaining pedagogies from Paris & Alim (2017), the goal was holding up the youth, responding to their needs and addressing the most pressing issues in their lives, privileging relationship building and the idea sharing emerging from this as the main goal, with multiple affordances of art as the guide along the way.

Youth Empowerment and Systemic Functional Linguistics

Jennings, Parra-Medina, Messias, and McLoughlin (2006) suggest that "in the broadest sense, empowerment refers to individuals…and communities gaining control and mastery, within the social, economic, and political contexts of their lives, in order to improve equity and quality of life" (p. 32). The pursuit of this empowerment drives a great deal of work in YPAR which, like its progenitor, participatory action research, "is distinct in its focus on collaboration, political engagement, and an explicit commitment to social justice" (Brydon-Miller, Kral, Maguire, Noffke, & Sabhlok, 2011, p. 387). One of the difficulties in the work, though, lies in power differentials that are inherent both in adult/youth relationships, but also, in this case, in those relationships as they play out in a school space and across racial and ethnic lines.

We may have wanted to see our CS SFL course as a play camp, different from regular 'summer school' with its punitive connotations. However, because it took place in a school building—most of the time—with adults who seemed pretty teacher-ish to our kids (read: mostly White, old-ish and either studying to be teachers or having taught in the past), we were all navigating swirling discourses that guided youth reactions to content and to people. We were trying to support "youth contributions to positive community development and sociopolitical change, resulting in youth who are critical citizens, actively participating in the day-to-day building of stronger more equitable communities" (Jennings et al, 2006, p. 40). Yet we have come to understand that this work may include youth resisting the modes through which that work might, originally, have been planned and orienting toward other modes that remain in the interstices of the manifest curriculum (Literat, 2013). The key is that the environment is rich with modal resources that participants can remix in whatever ways make the most sense in thinking about the changes or resistance they want to convey.

What we must stress, then, aligns with Hasan's (1996) view that: "literacy in the sense of untutored quotidian language development without the intervention of official pedagogy is already complex enough" and also a "social act of immense consequence" (p. 386). In other words, the relationship building and communication between youth and adults were already complex practices that deserved full attention. Indeed, this complexity lies in the fact that any "communicative event entails simultaneous use of multiple modes which may realize meanings that complement, extend, and/or contradict each other" (Early, Kendrick, & Potts, 2015, p. 448). In other words, although we planned a curriculum that asked young people to think about community change using various artistic affordances (photography, poetry, mapping, walking tours, community interviews), complex relationship building and resistance to that curriculum, in its many forms, was an important affordance. Resistance required shrewd, measured decisions on the part of youth and adult co-researchers. The failure we began to see, then, wasn't necessarily a total collapse of the curriculum, but was rather a movement whereby the young people chose their media; they only get there, though, because they are afforded the space, under the guidance of a few thoughtful adults, to try out various modes and registers.

One of the celebrated features of Systemic Functional Linguistics is its "focus on innovation, redesign, and subversion of genres" especially as related to the development of critical social literacy (Humphrey, 2018, p. 52). What this means in practice, clearly, varies immensely, but it requires of researchers (and co-researchers and teachers and youth workers in particular) a will to open up to possibility for change. One of the (very many) salient critiques of the standardization that has enveloped schooling in the last 30 years of creeping reform(ation) has to do with its inability and unwillingness to adapt to divergent youth needs[1]; we'd add to this, a bit altered, that it fails in disallowing youth to adapt it themselves. The difference is subtle, but it's a shift from something being done on behalf of youth to a process that is youth initiated.

What we see in Heidi's following narrative is very much youth-initiated redesigning and subversion of linguistic traditions and curricular intentions. That we saw ourselves as providing some manner of 'free' curriculum that 'enabled' youth to discuss their communities critically through various media still required, at least initially, an imposition of the media on the youth. The "untutored quotidian" shifts that the youth chose to make, in testing the boundaries of their relationships with Heidi—as well as, later, with another adult Stephanie and the art in the Museum—is a paramount example of the ways in which context matters, language variation equity matters and autonomous choices in configuring meaning matters (Harman, 2018). The point is: Given the chance, the girls took up multimodal resources differently than planned, but Heidi through her relationship with the youth was able to respond with an openness that led creative conclusions to emerge. This is, in a way, a tacit argument for a more flexible school curriculum, certainly, but also a plea for the space for teachers (and others) to get to spend time with kids on their own terms, in spaces they use, working on problems (even when they're not really working on problems) with their own texts, media and linguistic tools.

Narrative 1: Making/Taking Space for Exploration

During the first few days of camp, all the assigned groups get moved around, as kids flatly refuse to be separated from friends or find an adult they feel particularly connected to. At the end of the shuffle, I've got three girls in my group: Nya, Kally and Jory. I know Nya and Kally, who are in eighth grade, from the previous summer, but Jory, a seventh grader, is new to me. I also have, initially at least, an agreement with another adult to pair with her group of three girls on most assignments. We try. We really do. We set up competitions with the group of boys who have taken over the main meeting space. They fizzle. We try to give the larger group of girls video cameras to interview each other. Some of the younger girls use the opportunity to video themselves fighting—first playfully, but then with increasing intensity—as they first imitate a popular TV show and then rediscover old grievances left over from the school year. My group of girls has little patience for the younger girls, the community-based curriculum, with anything, really, that's going to feel like school and not summer: "We did this last year, Heidi! Why do we gotta do it again?"

At the beginning, too, they have very little patience with me. When I'm performing my version of caring adult, they interpret me as a fake. I often review our conversations on my drive home with burning cheeks as I think about the ways they call me on my bullshit: "Heidi, why did you say you are worried about your daughter being sold into sex slavery if she's on Snapchat? That's racist. You shouldn't talk about slavery like that." They catch me out, constantly, as I perform caring—as Whiteness, most often—in ways that create a distance that feels artificial. They insist that I enter their space as an authentic person, always, and I discover that the teacher persona I consistently carry with youth may exist first and foremost to protect me and my feelings rather than as a bridge toward understanding or respect.

In those first days, I try to engage the group in the art responses that are part of the curriculum. We embark on a spectacularly ho-hum photovoice walk, taking pictures of things that remind us of community, the girls complaining about the heat and the lameness of summer camps throughout. Following the curriculum, we dutifully move inside to remix one of our pictures in another art form. We flounder. We flop. We go through the motions. The girls are more interested in trading flirtatious barbs with the group of boys than they are in creating art that communicates anything about community. I sigh and bribe them with Oreos. I spend a lot of time on my drive home thinking about what needs to be done differently to make this meaningful for the girls.

After the first week, I make a decision to almost completely separate my group from the other campers, in the hopes that we can escape what feels like chaos. I also make a decision to scrap huge parts of the suggested curriculum of discussions around community (at least directly), and instead, we talk about feminism—a topic that I'm exploring in my own study and my own life—what it means to be a woman, what it feels like to be a young girl in middle school. And although I am not Black, we talk about what is unique about being a Black girl and being a Black woman because for these girls these are inseparable elements of their identity: "How would I know how it's different to be a White girl? I've never been one! *You* should tell *me* how it's different." I bring in music videos like Beyonce's "Lemonade" and they counter with music videos from Kodak Black. We watch them over and over and talk about the images of women, dissect the lyrics and connect the videos to the girls' lives.

We find classrooms that no one else is using. I ruthlessly tell other kids that we're doing our own thing and they need to go back to their own groups. I learn about these girls. I know, for example, that Nya plays basketball, but I also know who she has a crush on. I know about her mom, her family that lives 30 minutes away, and I know that she is a gifted and deeply funny mimic as she slyly imitates the sorority girls she sees around town, members of her family and me. I know that she gets in trouble at school because when she feels like she isn't being treated with respect—she can't help but speak out.

I come to know Kally, too—almost six feet tall in her stockinged feet—a volleyball player and the ultimate cool girl. She is the yin to Nya's yang, calm and collected and for the most part, able to talk Nya off the edge in classes they share. She's from a religious family and reluctantly shows me videos of her at church performing mime dancing. She seems surprised when I'm fascinated. She wants to go to college and then on to medical school so that she can become an anesthesiologist. She's the leader of our group, but that would be hard to know from the outside because she's not as outspoken as Nya.

Finally, I come to know Jory, who in some ways is in heaven—getting to be included with two of the cool girls who are a year ahead of her in school. But she quickly asserts the right to her own space in the group with her sheer intelligence and fearlessness in expressing her opinions. She listens carefully to what everyone says, but then she pushes her glasses up on her nose and says exactly what she thinks—whether you're going to like it or not. She has a boyfriend and she knows all the gossip from the middle school, and has a deep knowledge of the lives and relationships of celebrities who interest her. She is often the one who comes up with ideas that the other girls co-opt for the larger group. She's the one who writes the majority of the lyrics for the raps we compose together, and she also is the one who has the ideas for the visual art we end up creating together; more on both of these projects later. First it's worth spending time with the underlying theories that spurred the production of the course and, perhaps and probably, explain both its failures and the successes that the girls produce from the ashes of the initial curriculum.

Narrative 2: Stephanie P. Jones

It's the middle of camp, and the girls and I have successfully carved out a space and routine for ourselves, where we meet with the group in the first hour and then we wander the halls of the elementary school we're housed in until we find an empty, unlocked (hopefully cool) room and we take it over. Most days we lay on the floor, watch rap videos that allow us to discuss racism and feminism, tell stories, laugh and talk about everything from school gossip to celebrities. We scour websites that have sample beats from popular rap songs isolated, and we find the right track for the feminist rap that Jory wrote as a response to a piece of art at the state art museum (more on this later). We brainstorm sexist phrases we hear a lot—things like: "Imma tap that ass right there," because we want those phrases to be the recurring hook between verses and eventually settle on "Girl, make me a sandwich." They write another rap, joyfully, that ends every line with "bitch," a rap that they say is just for us (although they perform it over and over for fellow campers) because they know they won't be able to perform it at the end of camp celebration because the camp also includes elementary kids.

My contribution is access to my phone, and the wild, guttural laugh that happens when I'm fully supine, which they think is *hilarious*. I work hard (and mostly unsuccessfully) to mute my adult-ness while also providing the structural assistance they need to finish their lyrics, their visual art project, their community interviews and other projects that we are "supposed" to accomplish as part of the camp.

Perhaps my most important contribution is that I know and invite Stephanie P. Jones (Jones, 2015; Jones, 2018), a former graduate school colleague and a current university professor who specializes in Black girl literacies (Muhammad & Haddix, 2016), to join our group for one day. She graciously agrees, giving up a day of her summer vacation to drive a full hour and a half each way to come be with our group. We start the day with just two girls, because Nya is gone on a college campus visit with her sister, but within half an hour, we've picked up four more—who've drifted away from the larger group's yoga activity to join our group—and the room is full of energy.

I'm an observer here, watching a skilled practitioner and an experienced researcher at work. Stephanie's not talking sideways with the girls—she addresses them and listens to them in a way that leaves no doubt that she views them as people with interesting, funny and wise things to say about the world. She also refuses a version of adult caring that centers around control or containment. When the girls don't seem very enthusiastic about recapping the field trips and outings that the camp has provided, Stephanie shifts gears and invites them to tell stories and jot down phrases from their own narratives when the phrasing strikes them as interesting or important. Stephanie refuses to censor their thinking—when a girl tells a story (one that they clearly all know) about someone at school who is "giving head"—Stephanie matter-of-factly jots that phrase down on a paper, too. The girls, thus, construct found poems from their own stories—taping brightly colored strips of phrases they've said together in their own kind of wild tapestry of words and stories, which they then read out to each other. For at least one of the girls, this is the first "literacy event" in which I've seen her participate over the course of the camp thus far.

Watching Stephanie work is a joy and a master class, but I'm also a little bit envious. How come she can get this larger group to write poetry without complaint and I can't? How come I can only form deep relationships with the three girls in my group over the period of two weeks, and she does it in what seems like an instant with twice as many? Of course, the partial, but profound answer is that she's a Black woman working with Black girls and positionality matters. I agree with that—the girls in this group connected deeply to Stephanie because she understood intimately what it means to be a Black girl. But I also choose to refuse to sit with that answer because it releases me of responsibility to learn from the experience and reexamine my own pedagogy with youth of color. If the answer to why Stephanie is good at what she does with youth is simply that she's Black and so are they, then that feels, at best, dismissive of her as a practitioner and of (the) youth as learners. At worst, it's an excuse for White educators to disengage from relationship building with youth of color. What I take from this is a very clear snapshot of how culturally sustaining pedagogy (Paris, 2012) can be enacted in youth-centered spaces—using youths' own words as poetic and important, listening to stories without needing to shape them for the sake of respectability, letting youth talk with and over talk each other and inviting youth to create poetry (and art) while moving, talking and laughing.

Positionality and Culturally Sustaining Pedagogy

From this narrative, we wish to draw out two points: first, that both adult and youth positionality must be accounted for in shared learning spaces, and second, that culturally sustaining pedagogy is a vital part of critical, arts-based projects with youth.

What we mean here is that adults should enter youth spaces having examined and considered how their own positionality (in Heidi's case, a White woman working with Black girls) shapes their ability to interact with youth as they engage in critical work together. For Heidi, this meant remaining open to critique from the youth themselves about how her positionality as a middle-class White woman kept her from experiencing the world in the same way as the youth. It might mean that traditional power structures where the teacher is always the expert, always deserves respect, and is always right—or always needs to be right, at least—need to be challenged and reconfigured. Heidi's reckoning with the limits of her own positionality also meant that she created opportunities for youth to work with Stephanie, an educator whose positionality and pedagogy made different kinds of thinking and creating possible.

The second point here is that culturally sustaining pedagogy (Paris, 2012) can be learned and enacted by educators of *all* positionalities. Extending forward the work of Ladson-Billings (1995), Paris demonstrates that it is no longer enough for pedagogical practices to simply be responsive or relevant to the cultural experiences of our youth (p. 95). It is only through the sustaining of those cultural experiences of students and their communities—while extending their repertoire of dominant practices—that we can resist (and hopefully begin to repair) the erasure of marginalized youth language, literacies and cultural ways of being (p. 96). The lesson from Stephanie's visit then, is that yes, it might well have been the case that Stephanie's positionality invited a quick and easy familiarity with the girls as they recognized her as someone who understood them and had shared experiences with them. It is equally important, though, to recognize that although it took longer and felt messier (at least to Heidi), the girls in her group did end up trusting and connecting with her enough to make possible important critical moves in both their visual artmaking process and in their corresponding raps. We argue that centering culturally relevant and sustaining pedagogy in critical arts-based youth programs is the key to building the kind of trust between youth and adults that this work requires.

Narrative 3: Critical Visual Artmaking at the Museum

Every Tuesday we load the buses and drive 20 or so minutes to the local state art museum, where—thanks to a grant—we have access to the art collection, art materials, the museum's educational staff and space for creating our own art. The bus rides are my favorite: The whole bus will sometimes break out singing Bruno Mars' latest hit or the girls will look through the pictures on my phone and ask me questions about my family, my life, which I try to answer as honestly as possible.

Because we go every week, the process of creating visual art together reflects the shifting dynamics of our little group. The first week, for example, occurs as we were still attempting to follow the community curriculum of the larger group. We participate in a museum tour and each of the girls is tasked with finding a picture that reflects something about community to remix or riff off in their own artwork, which we work on together in the museum's classroom space. The girls gently resist the activity. Nya halfheartedly takes pictures of a few abstract pieces that she explains remind her of playing Nintendo because of the bright colors and the black lines that look like tangled controller wires. By the end of our allotted time touring the galleries, Kally still hasn't found a piece that she's interested in. And so I steer them in the direction of the traveling exhibit of Southern artists, hoping that something might speak to their life experience.

We are standing in front of a large, striking painting depicting lynching in the South when Jory asks, "Why would someone paint this?" I turn, ready to talk about the painting's commentary on racialized violence, only to find her puzzling over a canvas that is on a different wall. Nya and Kally gather round, too, and start to laugh. "Why'd someone draw a picture of some cows, but then who thinks a picture of cows should go in a museum?" Nya asks, her face comically skeptical.

The painting itself is of what appears to be a livestock auction. In the center of the canvas, an open-mouthed cow appears to be mid-moo, her eyes wild and focused directly on the viewer of the painting. A man leans against the railing that is fencing her in, and other faceless men in stadium seating seem to be judging this cow while several others are led into the auction area out of a cattle chute. The cows' hip bones are exaggeratedly jutting, adding to the sense of distress, but the men around the auction area seem more bored by the process than concerned about the cows.

Kally leans in for a closer look at the title and artist and says, "This doesn't even make sense! Why would you name it that?" The title placard reads: *The Male Gaze Reciprocated* (Casaletto).

"Ohhhhh," I say, "Probably to understand the title, I should tell you a little bit about how feminists use the term 'male gaze.'" I give them the briefest of overviews, and then they start to make the connections on their own. Jory starts: "So this painting is basically saying that women are treated like the cows in this painting?"

"That's messed up. They saying women are a piece of meat, right?" Nya shakes her head.
"Yeah, but it's saying it like the men are the ones doing something messed up, right, Heidi?"

Our interaction around the painting lasts maybe five minutes, but before we go, Jory snaps a picture of the painting: "I'm going to do this one instead of the other one I picked for that art project thing you're making us do." The interaction around this painting seems vital, somehow, and works to shift the focus of our group to something that the girls are interested in.

Our second week at the museum, we begin the remixing process using the art we selected as a jumping off point for our own art projects. I make it clear, and publicly, that I am an abysmal artist, and after my attempts to draw, no one bothers to disagree. Nya and Kally seem stumped and spend most of our time in the art studio painting their names, flowers and the sun. It turns out that Kally is a perfectionist, mercilessly throwing away any project that doesn't meet her approval (all of them, apparently). Nya blobs some color on a paper, draws some black lines on it and declares herself finished. Jory is sketching so lightly in pencil that I can't really tell what she's doing, but she slides her paper toward me and says, "Do you think this is what I'm supposed to do?"

A squat, square building dominates the drawing, bearing the title, "The Woman Factory" across its top and in smaller letters, "Created by Men and Society," and the road leading away from it has a sign pointing beyond the edge of the page titled simply "The World" (see Figure 7.1). As Jory shows Nya and Kally her drawing, all three of the girls begin to talk about the ways that they feel created by media, pop culture and their families. Jory and Kally talk about the pressure they felt to be high achievers because of an expectation for Black women to be strong and successful. Nya talks about how she gets in trouble at school because her (mostly White) teachers see her as a loud Black girl with a lot of attitude. At the end of this conversation, Kally looks at me and says, "You know we're all doing this project now, right?"

Our next few weeks at the museum are fun: We separate ourselves to our own corner of the art classroom space, we crank up classic TLC jams and we set to work. The girls expand the original concept of the woman factory by deciding to add two additional panels that they title "Inside the Woman Factory" which show women's bodies on a conveyor belt (see Figure 7.2). The bodies are cut out

FIGURE 7.1   The World

FIGURE 7.2   Inside the Woman Factory 1

FIGURE 7.3   Inside the Woman Factory 2

from mismatched fashion and celebrity magazines and as we cut out body parts, we talk. The girls notice that the only Black celebrity in the magazines we have is Solange Knowles, and we talk about how The Woman Factory is racist. We talk about what it means for them that most of the bodies that are portrayed as beautiful in mainstream society are White: "Heidi, you need to get us an *Essence* magazine to make us feel better, right?" Eventually, the bodies take shape, and the effect is slightly (and purposefully) grotesque: bodies that are mixed together out of proportion, emphasizing the big lips on one body, or the unrealistically skinny thighs of another (see Figure 7.3).

Conclusions

This chapter highlights the benefit of critical forays into visual art with youth—both as audience and artists. Importantly, youths' visual artwork informs and is informed by the work they do in other modalities: with writing their own rap, with writing poetry during Stephanie Jones's visit, with critiques of music and music videos. The girls see all of these pieces as part of the same project: understanding how they are positioned as Black girls and future Black women. Their purpose in creating art and performing their rap was to "reciprocate the male gaze" (as the title of the painting suggested) to speak back to the male gaze and to reclaim their identities for themselves. Vital, of course, to the entire process is trust. Irizarry (2018) puts it best, noting that "educational opportunities must be grounded in students' lived experiences, build on their systems of meaning-making, and provide students with the skills and confidence to advocate for themselves—indeed to sustain themselves and their communities" (p. 97). We get there, we think, certainly by remixing notions of relationship, possibility and curricular success (and failure); we get there through sustained relationships; we get there, particularly by providing the resources such that multiple registers open up a field of possibility for new critique and creation.

Praxis

Here we think about terms and activities that might support your work in a similar vein as that described in the chapter. Of course, as is the point of the chapter, some of these might be practices that youth reject or rework. This, we think, is a sign of active participation as much as resistance—and resistance as active participation!

Remixing. Revisioning and reimagining existing images opens space for youth interpretation and critical response in a low-stakes environment.

Link visual art and visual art responses to other modalities. Visual art can be a powerful way to process, talk about and represent student thinking. Linking visual art and visual art responses to other modalities (such as writing a rap, or analyzing music and lyrics) was an important part of the success of our project.

Make space for youth resistance in visual art. Part of the tradition of visual art is a tradition of non-conformity, abstract thinking, symbolic representation, etc. Making space for youth to join that tradition makes visual art a powerful medium for critical work. In some ways, this means adults take on flexible approaches to the final project and to the process of artmaking.

Avoid censoring, but encourage youth to consider audience and purpose. A prime example from this project might be in the way that the youth created a public rap with no language that might be viewed as objectionable to share with the rest of the campers (including children still in elementary school) but they created their own private rap with much more colorful language. Both raps spoke back to the male gaze, but the intended audience affected the register in which the youth wrote and performed.

To guide their thinking around audience and purpose (both in visual art and in writing), I used questions like:

- What's the intent behind using this word here?
- Who is the audience of this piece? What do you know about this audience and what they might already know about your topic?
- What message do you want the audience to take from this piece of art?

- Do you think that using this picture adds to your message or takes away from it?
- Who might object? Should they? Are you okay with them objecting?

Be open to your own learning process as an adult. Working with youth can be emotional, messy and personally uncomfortable, even while being rewarding. This project in particular demanded that the adults involved remained open to the possibility of being corrected by youth, being rejected by youth, even while learning from youth how to enter their spaces as a guide and a resource.

Note

1 Just as it creates, defines, labels and sanctions the very idea of divergence in the first place.

References

Brydon-Miller, M., Kral, M., Maguire, P., Noffke, S., & Sabhlok, A. (2011). Jazz and the banyan tree: Roots and riffs on participatory action research. In N. K. Denzin & Y. S. Lincoln (Eds.) *The SAGE handbook on qualitative research* (pp. 387–400). Thousand Oaks, CA: SAGE Publishers.

Early, M., Kendrick, M., & Potts, D. (2015). Multimodality: Out from the margins of English language teaching. *TESOL Quarterly, 49*(3), 447–460.

Gee, J. P. (1989). Literacy, discourse, and linguistics: Introduction and what is literacy? *Journal of Education Policy, 17*(1), 5–25.

Harman, R. (2018). Transforming normative discourses of schooling: Critical systemic functional linguistics praxis. In R. Harman (Ed.) *Bilingual learners and social equity: Critical approaches to systemic functional linguistics* (pp. 1–21). Cham, CH: Springer International.

Harman, R. (Ed.) (2018). *Bilingual learners and social equity: Critical approaches to systemic functional linguistics.* Cham, CH: Springer International.

Hasan, R. (1996). Literacy, everyday talk and society. In R. Hasan & G. Williams (Eds.) *Literacy in society* (pp. 377–424). London, UK: Longman.

Heath, S. B. (1983). *Ways with words: Language, life, and work in communities and classrooms.* Cambridge, UK: Cambridge University Press.

Humphrey, S. (2018). 'We can speak to the world': Applying meta-linguistic knowledge for specialized and reflexive literacies. In R. Harman (Ed.) *Bilingual learners and social equity: Critical approaches to systemic functional linguistics* (pp. 45–70). Cham, CH: Springer International.

Irizarry, J. G. (2018). 'For us, by us': A vision for culturally sustaining pedagogies forwarded by Latinx youth. In D. Paris & H. S. Alim (Eds.) *Culturally sustaining pedagogies: Teaching and learning for justice in a changing world* (pp. 83–98). New York, NY: Teachers College Press.

Jennings, L. B., Parra-Medina, D. M., Hilfinger-Messias, D. K., & McLoughlin, K. (2006). Toward a critical social theory of youth empowerment. *Journal of Community Practice, 14*(1-2), 31–55.

Jones, S. P. (2015). Taking it to the streets: A critical literacy approach to YA lit in the age of Michael Brown. Signal, Spring/Summer.

Jones, S. P. (2018). When it feels death, but it ain't: Spirit murder in all American boys. In M. Falter & S. Bickmore (Eds.) *Moving beyond personal loss to societal grieving: Discussing death's social impact through literature in the secondary ELA classroom* (pp. 35–46). Lanham, MD: Rowan and Littlefield.

Kittleson, J., Dresden, J., & Wenner, J. (2013). Describing the supported collaborative teaching model: A designed setting to enhance teacher education. *School-University Partnerships, 6*(2), 20–31.

Ladson-Billings, G. (1995). Toward a theory of culturally relevant pedagogy. *American Educational Research Journal, 32,* 465–491.

Literat, I. (2013). A pencil for your thoughts: Participatory drawing as a visual research method with children and youth. *International Journal of Qualitative Methods, 12*(1), 84–98.

Muhammad, G. E., & Haddix, M. (2016). Centering Black girls' literacies: A review of literature on the multiple ways of knowing of Black girls. *English Education, 48*(4), 299–336.

Paris, D. (2012). Culturally sustaining pedagogy: A needed change in stance, terminology, and practice. *Educational Researcher, 41*(3), 93–97.

Paris, D., & Alim, H. S. (Eds.). (2017). *Culturally sustaining pedagogies: Teaching and learning for justice in a changing world.* New York: Teachers College Press.

8

THEORETICAL REFLECTIONS ON THE AFFORDANCES AND CHALLENGES OF THE WORK

It will come as no surprise by this point in the work, that much of what we draw upon as we consider the work of conducting research and re/creating linguistic opportunities for expression and re/presentation with youth is rooted in transformative traditions of research. In this space we touch briefly—and again, but differently—on braided strands of humanizing research (Paris & Winn, 2014; Quiñones, 2015) and culturally sustaining pedagogies (CSP) (Paris & Alim, 2017) to reconsider notions of resistance and failure in our work. We note that when we "story over" (San Pedro, 2017, p. 101) the difficulties of the work—for researchers, for youth, for communities—in search of 'success' or, rather, a research narrative that fits the form of intervention to transformational change, we do an active disservice not only to our colleagues endeavoring to take up the work alongside us, but also of course, to the communities with which we hope to (continue to) work. As Tuck and Yang (2014) stated:

> Refusals are not subtractive but are theoretically generative...expansive. Refusal is not just a 'no,' but a redirection to ideas otherwise unacknowledged or unquestioned. (p. 239).

The idea would be that part of the "worthiness [and] witnessing" (Paris & Winn, 2014, p. xiv) that we hope to embody, to take up, in our work that involves "reciprocity and respect" (p. xvi) means dealing with, thinking through, and publishing on the refusals, the resistance to this work. This is particularly valuable, we think, because failing to give account to refusal means failing to "turn the gaze back upon power, specifically the colonial modalities of knowing persons as bodies to be differentially counted, violated, saved, and put to work"

(Tuck & Yang, 2014, p. 241). And only publishing (or seeking to publish about) successful youth work—or more commonly aggressively sanding off the rough edges, the long days wandering around with kids in spaces where they actively resist the pedagogy and the modalities in the work—means reducing research "to a performance of inquiry in order to acquire legitimacy" (p. 236) often at a cost to the communities with whom we partner.

Systemic Functional Linguistics can help us here. If we think of the ways in which publication often drives research—the need to publish for advancement in a career, but also as a way to disseminate ideas about which we have developed a passion—we can consider the tension, the dialectic, between the tendency for 'success' stories to get written and the actual data that emerges in youth-engaged projects. This "dialectic relationship between language and society" (Achugar & Carpenter, 2018, p. 93) is conceptualized as producing "situational contexts… linguistically…through the correlative choices of lexico-semantic wordings that represent reality" (p. 93). That we choose, most often, to present the easily captured successes of our research—the murals created; the parks built; the meetings in which youth took charge amongst city leaders—is, in many ways, an outgrowth of a genre of academic publication that has elided the value of characterizing difficulty, failure and refusal as social situations that emerge in youth arts research. Because a "language system is a meaning potential that is validated by a community" (p. 94) the larger community of youth research—those who conduct it; those who publish successfully about and around it—has tended to validate the meaning of activist youth research under the rubric of mostly easy wins, or struggles overcome. Again, we want to be very clear that in recognizing the splinter in others' eyes we are deeply aware of the beams in ours; this is a discourse, a register, to which we have contributed and from which we have benefited. The point that Tuck and Yang are making, however, is that this is inherently a colonizing practice as it socializes future researchers entering into the work to seek out success, to only tell of success and to either avoid failures—by avoiding risk, where valuable work might be done—or to avoid telling of them. Thus, community voices are appropriated in ways that reproduce a genre of success, uncritically, that makes light of the very real struggles of the work, but also of the community making sense of the work, and often rendering it not worth their time. It also means narrowing visions of success; for in many cases the ability to resist and refuse, properly acknowledged and honored, means something is working, even if the 'intervention' we'd hope to chronicle falls by the wayside.

CSP (Paris & Alim, 2017) suggest that "we must pay attention to both the liberatory and nonliberatory currents within" cultural "practices" (p. 11). In this case, we think it's vital to attend to the ways in which looking to failure, to refusal on the part of our research subjects, selves and situations—rather than failing to look in its direction, to theorize it, to write it and deal with it—might offer different liberatory possibilities in our work. This is especially vital because CSP calls researchers and teachers to think about how we "understand that the ways in which young people are enacting race, ethnicity, language, literacy, and their engagement with cultures is always shifting and dynamic" (p. 7). To story over this dynamism is to take the agency of refusal away from our research subjects and partners. We hope, in this chapter anyways, to fail to fail in this way.

What Might This Look Like?

Halberstam (2011) suggests that "under certain circumstances failing" among other diversions from traditional measures of success, "may in fact offer more creative, more cooperative, more surprising ways of being in the world" (pp. 3–4) in large part because "failure preserves some of the wondrous anarchy of childhood and disturbs the supposedly clean boundaries between adults and children" (p. 4). To learn to resee failure—in this particular case, as related to youth activist research—would require that we "untrain ourselves so that we can read the struggles and debates back into questions that seem settled and resolved" (p. 11). This cuts, at least initially, two ways in particular for our work here. The first has to do with generalized norms by which researchers present streamlined accounts of youth-engaged work that tell a progressive narrative—conditioned by manuscript-length constraints, but also normative practices within a field with a bias toward conclusions rooted in growth, progress and/or closure; the second has to do with our own limitations in conceptualizing youth creative praxis. That is: Our tendency, even in the midst of deep engagement with the theory with which we're working, has been to ignore, often, the ways in which "CSP...is about sustaining cultures as connected to sustaining the bodies—the lives—of the people who cherish and practice them" (p. 9). That our initial conceptualization of a community project, or curricular engagement, or co-researched project with youth—and especially with minoritized youth—might be resisted, altered, undermined or otherwise filigreed upon by the youth with whom we work is less an example of failure—except in our initial inability to recognize the failure of our own imaginations—than it is a production of a result. Or, more artfully: When kids choose to resist or refuse, this is theoretically expansive work that we'd do well to think along with. Given that prior research in *Culturally Sustaining Systemic Functional Linguistics (CS SFL)* holds that the work necessarily "fosters opportunities for minoritized students to transgress dominant spaces and fill them with vigorous expressions of their lived experiences and subjugated histories" (Khote, 2018, p. 157), youth resistance is not failure, but a taking up of critique, in various forms, that we'd do well to consider, write about and pass along through the critical youth research community.

Indeed, active listening and opening to what our youth and adult members are saying through resistance and creative remixing supports a shift to ontological presence in the work. As San Pedro (2017) stated,

> Hearing, seeing, and feeling the visual and verbal stories of others—and having their stories valued and validated by another—fosters a...community in which future discussions of race, colonization, and oppression can be discussed meaningfully and dialogically. (p. 112)

And so we've chosen, in this space, to flesh out the complications of working with youth. This isn't to impugn youth as difficult or disruptive, but to suggest that from among the many options available to them in a given space, even one that might be in some ways characterized as liberatory, youth sometimes refuse, they opt out, they lash out. And for good reasons mostly. The initial case comes from a summer program described in detail in previous chapters, which paired middle school youth and graduate students as co-researchers and co-participants in an arts-based curriculum meant to elucidate kids' sense of community and build capacity for driving social change. The program took place in a middle school building—one that many of the youth attended during the school year—as well as in the official art museum of the State in which the research was conducted. We discovered in the work many interesting things but certainly, by the end, couldn't say if we'd made much actual headway in relation to youth taking up art as a weapon for social change. Instead, mostly, we just muddled around with kids doing mundane things in mundane—although culturally and historically loaded spaces—often evoking, for youth, the kind of drudgery of regular school that we'd hoped to avoid in our work with them.

Summer 2016

Nine graduate students and 15 middle schoolers took part in this 2016 CS SFL program. The youth participants were all Black and from neighboring communities, save one Chinese newcomer. The adults were majority White, with only two Black graduate students among us. Informed by a YPAR approach, the paired graduate and middle school learners were to have collaborated each day through five inquiry modules that culminated in a community performance: (a) digital storytelling (taking photographs and sharing stories about their lives in the city), (b) architectural modeling (building ideal and real communities with blocks), (c) fiction (reading stories that resonate with youth lives), (d) theater role-playing and games (enacting a lived experience and discussing with the group) and (e) weekly visits to a museum to "interact" with formal art in a space beyond the school. The aim was to use these modalities that each pair of adult and youth co-researchers might explore and represent dreams and stories about their lives and community (e.g., the need for youth art space in the city).

The degree to which youth engaged across activities, however, varied wildly. Some of our youth members perceived any activities such as reading young adult fiction or discussing short videos as belonging to their understanding of the dull and oppressive regimes of school. At those times when they read the space as strictly connected to school activities, they often reclaimed the space by engaging in boundary-exploring resistant behavior (like jumping on the backs of adult researchers; yelling for the sake of testing their voices; breaking and throwing crayons at facilitators) and important acts of self-assertion about who they were and what they wanted from their communities. They were, in other words, translating the supposedly 'freer' space of our time together into a harmful place of remembered-self-at-school. Resistance allowed them to move into imaginary and playful distance from work that felt too close to schoolish and, thus, punitive. Resistance to literacy activities in several of our CS SFL programs also taught us how damaging the routinized literacy activities in school could be to youth whose desire to read or write was dampened by teaching to test regimes, among other largely hidden forces.

In the school including the classroom, the hallways, and the gym as well as in the museum's art studio and galleries, youth reacted to their surroundings in complex manners—shifting their ways of being to reclaim a space for themselves or to resist practices in a space where they felt decidedly unwelcome. Indeed, several youth reclaimed the hallways of the school, a highly regulated space during the regular academic year, as their own imaginary play space. Several students appropriated the rolling of teacher chairs from classrooms and pushed each other up and down the hallway in them. Zira, a lively sixth grader who generally declined to participate in any activities that involved adults, did however recruit an adult researcher to repeatedly push her up and down the hallway. Those rolling chairs, which were normally reserved for teachers and other adults in positions of power, were reclaimed by the youth as objects of play and, in Zira's case, to assert her own position of power in relation to the adult researchers. The central lesson of the work, though, was: Given the chance to opt out of activities, youth may in fact choose to opt out, no matter how well constructed or interesting adults may think that they are. The tension of the work, then, particularly in a highly regulated space like a school, even in a summer environment where some rules are relaxed, lies in figuring out how to be with youth when adults aren't setting the explicit curricular terms of interaction.

Interestingly, in theater scenarios, when they chose to reenact classroom conflicts with overbearing or racist teachers, the students amplified the pitch, gestures and actions of teachers in comic and also highly focused ways. A number of our youth co-researchers, resistant to the versions of themselves reflected in a feeling of 'school' emanating from traditional literacy activities, were ready to critique the situations of their lives that produced them as 'bad' students by enacting, sardonically and passionately, the roles of racist teacher or resistant student in skits focused on elucidating their experiences of school. Their resistance to 'reading' came from negative experiences as readers in school, but also enabled them to produce—to read and write as it were—symbolic representations of the structures of school that limited and labeled them as non-readers. Similarly, Heath (1983) found that minoritized youth who did not see themselves as strong students in school settings excelled in improvising and writing their own scripts for community performances. Heath noted that, "once these actors became their own authors, they seemed to tap in performance a deep range of linguistic competence that they otherwise did not display" (p.80). This was certainly true of a young woman, Zambika, with whom we worked who showed an elastic versatility in improvising the prosodic and gestural contours of the principal, 'bad' student or teacher.

Zambika

Zambika is an energetic, assertive, Black girl. Every day of that summer her hair was styled differently: Some days she wore it loose, other days it was braided tightly or in an Afro-puff, and still other days it was straightened. In some ways, Zambika's hair could serve as a metaphor for the young woman herself: She was perhaps the most skilled of the youth in examining and transforming the social boundaries of the spaces around her and responding accordingly. In our daily meeting room at the school, she used her booming voice to command the attention of (and sometimes to literally command) her peers and the adult researchers. Davvy, Zambika's adult co-researcher, recorded her thoughts in her field notes:

> I think she understands that she's not really ... that she's almost playing a part ... that these things that she does like throwing crayons and leaving the room and stuff, that those are just things that she does in order to deflect—those are just parts that she plays. I think she's very aware of those as just parts.

In the more highly controlled museum space, Zambika expressed anger toward the adults in the museum whom she perceived (rightly, we think) as always looking at her in a negative way. In this space, she took on a resistant role, moving to stand behind a museum docent as she gave her presentation (making the museum worker decidedly uncomfortable) or walking just past signs that asked museum patrons not to enter certain rooms. Another of the adult researchers recorded Zambika's resistance in the museum space in her field notes:

> Zambika in particular is fascinating in the ways that she purposefully (I think, anyway) comes right up against the edge of the rules, and even

steps one foot over just to dare someone to say something: like when she moved further into the vault, crossing past the curator and giving her the bunny ears as she moved to stand somewhere different from where she was "supposed" to be was kind of a master class in subversion. When the exhibits were closed, too, she walked two steps past the sign saying "CLOSED" and just waited for someone to come fetch her. I don't think she really cared if she went back there or not, but she sure as hell cared that people saw her subverting those dominant norms. That girl has guts.

During a tour of the archives of the museum, Zambika was visibly upset to find two carefully archived oil paintings that depicted a group of enslaved people "happily" working under the benevolent eyes of White men. After fidgeting visibly, ignoring the ongoing formal presentation that the bulk of her peers were more or less attending to, she asked, "What is this doing here? This isn't art." When a museum staff member explained that it had been pulled off of a community center wall in a local town because of its overtly racist depiction of enslaved people and masters, Zambika was not placated. She began to make slashing motions at the painting (as if she held a knife). She expressed several times that the painting should not be preserved in a museum[1]. In light of this response to the art in particular and her mood of rebellion in the museum in general, her actions could be read as a resistance to what she felt was the consistent message that she, as a Black girl, didn't matter in that space, that the history of slavery and racist depictions of that egregious past could be accepted as legitimate objects of art. It also could be read as her understanding of the function of our youth and adult space: With her allies, we, the adult university-based co-researchers, she felt emboldened to take on the authorities in highly visible and resistant ways.

Indeed, in several performed scenarios during the course of our time together, Zambika reveled in assuming the role of authoritative school figures with a seamless move into their modulated prosody, gestures and verbiage. Similarly, on field trips, the adults asked Zambika to be responsible for the smaller children on tours, and she easily assumed a role of responsibility, maturity and "teacher-ness." In an "I Am" poem that Zambika completed, she highlighted her capacity closing with the statement: "I understand the world." The co-researchers who worked with Zambika agreed with her self-assessment: She demonstrated an uncanny ability to read the world around her and adjust her own way of being to resist, affirm or transform the situations in which she found herself. That is: Zambika read places as performative opportunities in and through which she could take on different versions of herself. Indeed, in her discussions with her co-researchers regarding her caring role with the younger students, she noted that she didn't want them to grow up to be like her. In this case, she was re-encoding a label from her time in schools where her resistance was perceived as indicative of an inherent inability and unwillingness to be 'schooled.'

Our attempts to allow Zambika spaces to play different roles safely and without sanction were, at best, half achieved and led to deep debates about whether and if we were doing a disservice to a young Black woman in particular, by letting her flout rules with us that might get her in trouble with other adults in our absence. We've never entirely squared that circle, so to speak, and would suggest that any work with youth—and particularly with youth of color—has to consider the implications of the possibilities we seek to open up in the heterotopic (Foucault, 1986) or carnivalesque (Bakhtin, 1998) spaces of youth action and participatory research. That is: One concern is that in our seeing Zambika as fully aware of her ability to change roles and manipulate spaces purposefully, we might well be reinscribing larger racial narratives that ascribe adult characteristics to Black children in particular, functionally taking away their childhood and the innocence that is presumed of their (White) counterparts (e.g., Jenks, 1996). In other words, our reading and celebration of Zambika in this chapter and in our relationship with her could itself be influenced by our own privileged understanding of YPAR space as one that opens and celebrates divergent and oppositional thinking and being. In the white ivory towers of our university, we can wear our jeans and put our feet on the table in faculty meetings but can Zambika, a young underserved youth, enjoy such freedom outside of our short times together in the summer? Our work in an afterschool program with youth provides some context to our thinking about Zambika and the issue of loving critique as it emerges in CSP.

Afterschool CS SFL Programs

Working within a school context during the regular school year, even if it was in an afterschool program, allowed a whole other set of issues to emerge from those that were present in our summer programming. In our research on our afterschool programs (Harman, Siffrinn, Mizell & Bui, in press) we found several challenges caused by our own limits in building an adequately permeable curriculum for our middle school youth, impatient to move out of the restrictive spaces of the school halls, cafeteria and desk-to-front powerpoint screen orientation. The institutional practices of the school also affected the impact our CS SFL programs could have. As described at length in Chapters 1 and 2, the program offered adult and youth participants with a playful space where theater games, drawing activities and hip hop workshops supported them in inhabiting the space in less hierarchical and more agentive ways. At times youth played the role of leaders, at times the adult members led the activities. We focus here, on the difficulties related to one young student, whose approach to the work was accommodated within the program up to its institutional limits. Progress, marked through journal entries of a veteran teacher, only meant so much in the absence of decision-making power at the level of the school.

Yona

Yona is a passionate and expressive young girl. She is also a very independent player. In our program, she tended to prefer not to join our play activities but instead found an alternative space where she would interview friends or adults about her subject of the day. Some of the adults in our group found Yona's resistance to working on joint projects very difficult. She did not intend to follow anyone for the sake of compliance but instead showed she wanted to be with us, but in her own way. One seasoned educator observed the following:

> Jason came over and gave Yona a camera and later exchanged it for a video camera. I'd like to reflect on this for a moment and maybe later ask Jason his reasoning (I'm in no position to question, just wondering): I realize Yona does not have a good attention span and this tactic is perhaps to help her stay in touch and a part of the group, but I found it confusing (to be honest). It seems that it gives her "permission" to do something different than everyone else. Her pictures and video, to my knowledge, are not being used for this project, so I don't understand the exact purpose. While we mapped and filled out the survey, she couldn't do that because she held a camera. Just some thoughts about my confusion, because I do not know a great deal about middle schoolers!

Jason and Ruth sometimes found Yona's desire to be part of an outgroup difficult. However, they developed a trusting relationship with her that indicated that we were in an improvisational space where her use of the camera or space could lead to different outcomes, different remixing of modalities. The same veteran teacher, Vanessa, talked about her relating with Yona differently later on in the mapping module:

> Finally, Yona was participating. We all took pictures so we can re-create next week. But when Fiona demolished it, Yona ran out. Foxy said to me, "She'll be okay, just give her a minute. She does that sometimes." I asked her if she thought I should go to her and she said that would be okay. So I went out and Yona was just right outside the door. I asked her if she was okay and she replied, "I just wanted to play some more." I assured her that we would next week and that unfortunately our time had run out. She agreed and came back in.

What is important in this reflection on the part of Vanessa is it shows how she is moving from a binary view of Yona and her practices and instead actively listening and responding to Yona in that moment and time. From our research of the adults in our programs, many similar to Vanessa began to shift the way they viewed relationship building with youth.

At times, though, as a Black parent and community member, Jason would speak directly to Yona if she disrupted the group work that was happening. As Paris and Alim (2017) discuss, we needed to signal when youth or adult practices were not supporting collaborative negotiation of the space. Significantly, however, our deepening relationship with Yona was very different from her relationship with many teachers and administrators at the school. Two days before the end of our program, Yona was banned from coming to work with us. We were chagrined by this as the final legislative theater performance was to be held in front of the principal of the school. As a highly energetic and vocal performer, Yona would have thrived in sharing her vision for a new youth lounge in the school. As facilitators of an afterschool program, we had no power to ask for an exception to their disciplinary measure, meted out for some other reason that did not have anything to do with our program.

This case study of Yona highlights how often lacking in our afterschool and summer programs is full institutional support (school board, middle school or university administration) in terms of an adequate place to work with students, supplies, uninterrupted time to work, transportation to bring youth to the university campus and other places, and collaborative exchanges with content area teachers who work with our youth everyday but who rarely have the time to cooperate with us in our programs. All of these limitations take away from the time we can spend effecting change in institutions that our youth participants bring to our attention.

Parkside Center

One of the lessons that we've learned in our work, and this emerges consistently in humanizing research, is that relationships, properly conceived, require time. At the end of our time in the summer with the youth we write about above, we followed the lead of a student who suggested that we might be able to reopen a community center in her public housing complex to turn it back into a community space again in service of kids in particular. This led us to approach the local housing authority; the agency was kind enough to grant us access to the building and accommodating enough to make resources available that we might provide programming in partnership; that is: Our department would build academic programming for the community and the housing authority would provide infrastructural support (e.g., heat, cleaning supplies, internet, etc.). Fresh Memorandum of Understanding (MOU) in hand—annually renewable at the behest of the housing authority—we set off on the work of building trust in the community which is home to upwards of 250 families, most of whom are African-American and the lion's share of whom live well below the federal poverty line. There are any number of missteps we might share related to the pulls of time on faculty life that meant we weren't in the Center as often as we would have liked, but still, we took the time—a full year, in fact—conducting charrettes, meeting parents and kids, throwing opening parties and applying, constantly, for funding to support the work. We built relationships and worked toward trust with the residents surrounding the community center and thought, in some sense, that our work was on its way and rooted in honest engagement with culturally sustaining principles. Still, while we focused on the neighborhood, on the people in the community, we missed a vital component: the relationship with the housing authority to whom we report.

Embedded within the MOU was language related to accountability. Essentially we were to keep the housing authority apprised of any time we were in the Center and provide some cursory analysis of the relative attendance and 'success' of any given initiative. We had to report out. We also had to take on the responsibility of conducting and collecting background checks on any university-affiliated volunteer in the space; as well, we were responsible for providing fungible resources in the space (art supplies, mostly, but also athletic equipment and books…lots of books). As community-focused researchers and former teachers, these were not necessarily tasks wholly out of our various competencies, but they were certainly time and energy consuming in addition to our full-time commitments to coursework, research projects, service and, of course, our family obligations. In short: We were stretched really thin and made decisions—consciously or otherwise—to attend to some things and not to others. These decisions had consequences we hadn't expected in the excitement of following through on a YPAR project.

We're reminded, in writing this of Randy Stoecker's admonishment that in community work when a "researcher refus[es] to build trust with the research subject, the research subject" might choose to withhold information from the researcher (2013, p. 6). Here we'd made a mistake of forgetting that we were in a three-way relationship. All of the diligent work we were undertaking to carefully build trust—especially as most of us are White researchers trying to be careful in the wake of colonizing strains in activist research—with community members should have been omnidirectional. It wasn't that we were neglecting to report to the housing authority what we were doing, but that what we were doing didn't match neatly with the kinds of metrics that might have been recognizable and we never took the time to help the housing authority understand both the underlying theories of the work nor the difficulties in getting it up and running for the long term. And so, when the MOU came up for renewal we faced the very real possibility that we'd lose access to the community center and that we'd end up pushed out of the community, confirming for the residents what we'd hoped to avoid in all of our relationship building work—that we'd just leave, as had others from the university, from the research community, when we'd gotten what we wanted. Cut to a very tense afternoon where Kevin spent most of his down time while running a teacher professional development in another state, trying to track the status of the MOU as it bounced around a meeting in Georgia, at risk of being struck down. This was on top of a second MOU that was meant to build a new partnership with the medical school in town where beginning medical students would, potentially, be working in a community health course in the community center as a way to bolster residents' access to health care, and strengthen early medical school education around holistic factors related to clinical care. We were, in essence, on the hook for our own research mistakes of course, but also because the medical school faculty had trusted us, and we were about to catastrophically disrupt the first semester of a group of eight medical school students.

In the end things worked out. Temporarily. We bought ourselves another year. In the midst of the final revisions of this manuscript we made a determination, based on the further deterioration of the relationship, to withdraw from the partnership with the housing authority. This was particularly difficult given that we'd developed deep relationships with residents and youth in the community and had built a string of relationships with service providers (the local diaper bank; the school district social worker; faculty members across our college) to improve both the lives of the members of the community and the experience of the volunteers and faculty in the space. But ultimately we failed in constructing a tenable partnership. As we search for a new place to replant our work, we remain committed to extending the relationships already begun, but in the end, we just don't know what will happen next. This has us alternating between despair, anger, and sadness at having let our youth partners down.

We draw attention to the challenges, failures and insights that have emerged in our struggles to establish community or summer programs also to support others interested in doing this work. We do not want to dishearten anyone from taking up the work. We find it highly rewarding in terms of our developing understanding and relationships with vibrant communities that are so often invisible, unheard within the dominant discourses of urban planning, schools and social networks. However, we also urge ourselves and others to allow for improvisation to be a key part of any work carried out with community stakeholders. We are neither the subject nor the driving force of the programs but as Yancy (2008) emphasizes, it is youth that need to be full center of the work. That means relinquishing our desire for control over how programs, relationships and agendas develop. Instead, with active listening and waiting, the community leads us to where we need to go.

Note

1 We don't engage with the ethics of preserving problematic art in this volume, although it is worth noting that the museum in question is the official museum of a Southeastern State and so is beholden to a number of different ideological directives.

References

Achugar, M., & Carpenter, B. D. (2018). Critical SFL praxis principles in English language arts education: Engaging pre-service teachers in reflective practice. In R. Harman (Ed.) *Bilingual learners and social equity: Critical approaches to systemic functional linguistics* (pp. 91–108). Cham, CH: Springer International.

Bakhtin, M. (1998). Carnival and the carnivalesque. In J. Storey (Ed.) *Cultural theory and popular culture* (pp. 250–258). Athens, GA: University of Georgia Press.

Foucault, M. (1986). Of other spaces. *Diacritics, 16*(1), 22–27.

Halberstam, J. (2011). *The queer art of failure.* Durham, NC: Duke University Press.

Harman, R., Siffrinn, N., Mizell, J., & Bui, K. (in press). Promoting reflection literacy in pre-service language teacher education: Critical SFL praxis with multilingual youth. In L. Altariste & C. Crosby (Eds.), *Second language writing across PK16 contexts: Intersections of teaching, learning, and development.* Ann Arbor, MI: University of Michigan Press.

Heath, S. B. (1983). *Ways with words: Language, life, and work in communities and classrooms.* Cambridge, UK: Cambridge University Press.

Jenks, C. (1996). *Childhood.* New York: Routledge.

Khote, N. (2018). Translanguaging in systemic functional linguistics: A culturally sustaining pedagogy for writing in secondary schools. In R. Harman (Ed.) *Bilingual learners and social equity: Critical approaches to systemic functional linguistics* (pp. 153–178). Cham, CH: Springer International.

Paris, D., & Winn, M. T. (Eds.). (2014). *Humanizing research: Decolonizing qualitative inquiry with youth and communities.* Thousand Oaks, CA: SAGE Publications.

Paris, D., & Alim, H. S. (Eds.). (2017). *Culturally sustaining pedagogies: Teaching and learning for justice in a changing world.* New York, NY: Teachers College Press.

Quiñones, S. (2015). (Re)Braiding to tell: Using trenzas as a metaphorical-analytical took on qualitative research. *International Journal of Qualitative Studies in Education, 29*(3), 338–358.

San Pedro, T. J. (2017). "This stuff interests me": Re-centering indigenous paradigms in colonizing schooling spaces. In D. Paris & H. S. Alim (Eds.) *Culturally sustaining pedagogies: Teaching and learning for justice in a changing world* (pp. 99–116). New York, NY: Teachers College Press.

Stoecker, R. (2013). *Research methods for community change: A project-based approach.* Thousand Oaks, CA: SAGE.

Tuck, E., & Yang, K. W. (2014). R-words: Refusing research. In D. Paris & M. Winn (Eds.) *Humanizing research: Decolonizing qualitative inquiry with youth and communities* (pp. 223–247). Thousand Oaks, CA: SAGE.

Yancy, G. (2008). *Black bodies, white gazes: The continuing significance of race in America.* Lanham, MD: Rowman & Littlefield.

9

CS SFL PRAXIS AND EMBODIED INQUIRY: IMPLICATIONS AND CONCLUSIONS

In a lecture at the University of Georgia, Shirley Brice Heath (2018) reminded us all of the pivotal importance of engaging our young in dynamic interaction with language and text. Without extended language interaction, she said, children stumble and lack motivation to learn. In the current market-based approach to education (Kirshner & Jefferson, 2015), school closures, corrective educational strategies and high-stakes testing reflect a theory and practice of education that ignores the physical, emotional and conceptual knowledges of students (Rosenfeld Halverson, 2010). Indeed, routinized high-stakes testing practices most often foster a system where "young people are not viewed as legitimate stakeholders or participants in institutions that shape their lives" (Kirshner, 2010, p. 239). Instead, young people are most often minoritized, particularly youth of color (Kirshner, 2010; Rosenfeld Halverson, 2010). This erasure of the insights, fears and dreams of the young in school and community decision-making processes reifies institutional power dynamics (Kirshner & Jefferson, 2015), enacting policies and practices that constrain students from developing a critical understanding of social issues or participating critically in the public sphere (North, 2008, p. 1195).

With the goal of bringing diverse populations together to identify, study and address social issues relevant to local communities and schools (Cammarota & Fine, 2008), participatory and culturally sustaining approaches attempt to combat many of the deficits identified in traditional educational and research models. These innovative approaches aim to collapse boundaries that traditionally delineate categories such as teacher/student, youth/adult and researcher/participant by including youth in the research planning, decision-making processes and the presentation of research, with critical participation in the public sphere. This results in a more collaborative approach to educational change (Mitra, 2009). Informed by Freire's (1998) concept of praxis—that is the recursive connections between reflection and action—Youth Participatory Action Research (YPAR) positions students as active researchers and agents of change in their schools and communities (Cammarota & Fine, 2008). In this sociocultural approach to community research, youth engage in activities rooted in and relevant to the histories and cultures of their communities, where they know their voices matter (Duncan, 2002; Fisher, 2007; Kinloch, 2010, 2012; Kirkland, 2004; Lee, 2007). Within this YPAR framework, arts-based processes such as theater, poetry and architectural designing are used to generate collective action on and civic engagement in local community issues (e.g., Davis, 2009; Ginwright, 2008; Greene, Burke, & Mckenna, 2016; Kim, 2013). Through the use of theater, storytelling, social action and discussion, for example, minoritized bilingual and bidialectal youth use their academic and social Englishes and other languages to voice socio-political and cultural interests (Davis, 2009).

In this vein, culturally sustaining pedagogy (CSP) conceptualizes work with youth as "centered on contending in complex ways with the rich and innovative linguistic, literate, and cultural practices of...youth and communities of color" (Paris & Alim, 2014, p. 86). Our work in this book has been to support your understanding of how CSPs can be operationalized through an orchestrated curriculum of multiliteracies informed by Systemic Functional Linguistics (SFL) and its theories of social semiotics. SFL theory celebrates the "eco-social" nature of language that shifts to accommodate variation (Lukin, Moore, Herke, Wegener, & Wu, 2011, p.18). In connecting SFL and CSP, we could say that Halliday's theory promotes language variation equity and Paris and Alim's approach promotes cultural variation equity.

Our book provides exploration of this combined CSP and SFL work in complementary ways. Importantly, Chapter 3 provides the pivotal reason why CS SFL work is vital and why, despite our failures and embarrassing blunders, we continue to do, and believe deeply in, this work. Specifically, Jason Mizell, a Black bilingual community activist and university researcher, shares his own testimonio as to how his childhood and adult experiences of racism and linguicism, and deep appreciation for his mother and others in his community have motivated him to be a passionate CS SFL educator. The youth testimonios of Cierra, Simon and Edgar show how their intergenerational bonding and collaborative inquiry with Jason supported them to continue fighting for equity for others and themselves. All three youth remain vibrant members of our CS SFL Institute.

In Chapter 4, we have also seen how mapping and surveying can deepen inquiry about urban geography and community relationships in ways that a PowerPoint and a canned curriculum could hardly generate. Through use of the physical, spatial and visual domains of knowledge construction, participants begin to understand and challenge the status quo in their schools and cities. As

Kevin Burke describes, it was when youth members took them on a real tour of their environs that they began to share their insights, dreams and fears with the facilitators. In the case of school mapping and block building, as Khanh Bui explains, a shy bilingual girl configured use of the range of modal resources such as gesture, spatial layout and verbal discourse to explain her vision of a vibrant school to her community. In different but corresponding ways, Chapters 5 and 6 explore how play and movement support intergenerational groups to form different relationships, through experiences with language play and hip hop. Performance, as a culminating module in these programs, supports the group in mobilizing the diverse modal repertoires to argue for change and for imaginative revision of the normative practices of schooling. In Chapters 7 and 8, we see how our youth members are always ready to resist and transform what we have set up as the chosen curriculum or set of activities. We also discuss our constant failures in this work, failures that need to be expected in a system where we researchers hold a privileged position within our city and nation and where many of our youth researchers struggle to receive not only cultural sustenance but nutritional and affective nourishment from a broken system.

This final chapter provides an overview of the strengths and challenges of our CS SFL praxis, as discussed in this book, with implications for researchers and educators interested in this work.

Strengths of Our CS SFL Praxis

The CS SFL praxis discussed in this book comes from our experiences as facilitators and researchers of youth programs, primarily in the southeast of the United States. We define CS SFL praxis as an approach that validates and incorporates the cultural, multimodal, affective and linguistic repertoires of all program participants. Importantly, it also involves deliberate and sequenced incorporation of a wide and cumulative range of modes (e.g., mapping, drawing, role playing, joking, rapping) that can be remixed for different purposes and audiences. Figure 9.1 illustrates how the different curricular modules (e.g., mapping, storytelling, rapping, arguing, performing) activate use of an ever-widening range of modal resources.

CS SFL praxis, focused primarily on youth inquiry, supports youth and adults in moving through a recursive set of creative processes, dialogic and formal interactions and creative remixing of designs. In this 2017 program, participants engaged in mapping their school and then moved to building with blocks and paper a design of a new building or other resource they wanted to see added to the school (e.g., running track, lounge, shop). Finally, they were asked to argue for their new structure in a legislative theater event, where they used argumentation, design displays and persuasive embodied language to convince the administrators of the saliency of their project.

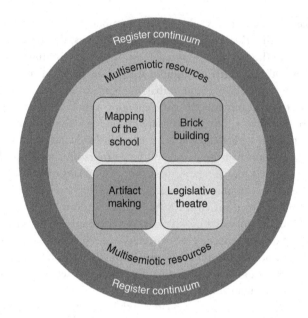

FIGURE 9.1 CS SFL Pedagogical Design

As illustrated in Figure 9.1, the sequence of modal activities is deliberate and meant to encourage youth and pre-service teachers to avail themselves of an expanding set of multi-semiotic resources to convey their insights, contribute new knowledge to the community of learning and reflect on community issues. In addition, the register continuum (from mapping and surveying the school to building with blocks) supports the group in shifting to a different field, tenor and mode in each module.

As the culminating module, legislative theater, for instance, is a complex verbal, physical and multimodal activity that requires deep understanding of the subject matter (the field), the audience (the tenor) and the organization of meaning (the mode). Instead of relying on power points and computer programs, our participants co-construct knowledge together, through dialogue and modalities, through research preparation and rehearsals. Andre, featured in Chapter 6, chose hip hop to persuade his principal of the importance of his ideas. His choice of this culturally validated and complex genre supported him in remixing his argument in rhythmic and rhymed prose. Similarly, Humphrey (2008) in her study of the discourse of young activists found that their "complex persuasive goals, social identities, roles and relationships in the civic domain necessitate the mobilization of an extensive repertoire of interpersonal resources at the level of genre and discourse semantics" (p. 295). By having the freedom to choose among a wide variety of meaning-making resources, Andre and his peers showed impressive understanding of how remixing of sound, movement and rhetoric resources could persuade an audience. Importantly, their adult co-researchers also supported this understanding through dialogue, co-construction of arguments and mentoring when needed.

Too often in contemporary classrooms, ironically, the digital age has placed huge importance on tapping, interacting with and processing computer programs, games and tests to the detriment of physical, affective and verbal engagement in embodied inquiry. Shirley Brice Heath (2015), as mentioned by Nicole Siffrinn in Chapter 6, warns us of the dangers of paying too little attention to the rich meaning-making resources of children and youth and their multiliteracies that involve movement, gesture, laughter and other modal and material resources. In our CS SFL programs, instead, youth and adults engage in research, art work and community outreach that pushes participants into new understandings and dimensions. For example, the community mural created by middle schoolers and graduate students under the expert guidance of a local muralist, Broderick Flanigan, grew out of an adult-youth research partnership centered in the Parkside Community Learning Center. Youth and their adult co-researchers spent time, through youth-guided community tours, freestyle rap battles, photographic walks and chalk-art sessions sussing out what would best represent that which was most valued and that which was most needed to change as the community moved forward. Kids were very clear that parking, represented by the congested road in front of the PCLC was a consistent problem for their parents, particularly on football game days in our university town; they were also emphatic that the people, represented in so many different forms by the youth artists, were the strength of the space.

Across the modalities, CS SFL facilitators use an embodied SFL-informed teaching and learning cycle (TLC) (Siffrinn & Harman, 2019). What this approach does is to try and incorporate the cultural, semiotic and material resources that youth and other participants bring to the program with the goal of remixing these resources to deepen conceptual understanding of civic literacy and advocacy (Potts & Moran, 2013). In the CS SFL-informed TLC, the first phase, referred to as *deconstruction,* supports learners in activating their cultural and multilingual knowledge base about the topic. In the second phase, called *joint construction*, students are encouraged to physically engage in inquiry around the topic while simultaneously verbally articulating their understandings with the active participation of peers and adult co-researchers. In the final stage of the cycle, students *apply* their understanding to a new scenario by performing in front of key stakeholders and preparing a well-balanced argument. This cycle of instruction and interaction can be used in classroom and community settings. Harman, Buxton, Cardozo-Gaibisso, Lei & Bui (in press), for example, discuss how this CS SFL approach can be applied to science classrooms in similar ways.

In addition, our work in the CS SFL programs has led to significant changes in how novice teachers perceive their teaching career. Indeed, in a recent study (Harman, Siffrinn, Mizell, & Bui, in press), a qualitative analysis of teacher reflections, curriculum design and subsequent instruction showed their passion, insights and determination to adopt a CS SFL approach to language and disciplinary learning. Similarly, Abu El-Haj and Rubin (2009) found that immersion in youth-oriented programs supported novice teachers in developing pedagogical designs more aligned with student needs and interests. In a more recent study, Rubin, Abu El-Haj, Graham, and Clay (2016) found that pre-service teachers engaged in youth programs were more likely to develop a social justice pedagogy "that goes beyond providing an equitable civic education, instead aiming to create transformative civic learning experiences that help students to interpret, resist, and creatively address the forces that affect their lives" (p. 434). In a combined program such as ours, the CS SFL approach supported teachers in moving toward a pedagogy of multiliteracies where the body, material and semiotic resources and affective involvement were seen as crucial to disciplinary meaning-making (Collier & Rowsell, 2014).

In their book about place-making with youth, Derr, Chawla, and Mintzer highlight the importance of creating programs that have the following elements: local and place-based; transparency and honesty; inclusive; relevant; sustainable; voluntary and playful. We very much adhere to these same principles in our work, emphasizing also, however, that the curriculum needs to be orchestrated so that our youth and adults build cumulatively in terms of discourse strategies (through moving across registers), knowledge generation (deepening of their knowledge of urban design and planning) and cultural sustenance (awareness that their repertoires are being integrated into the program). All of the modalities and activities serve as a powerful resource for multilingual students to stand up for their rights and education (Humphrey 2010).

Limitations

Because our work is always just a beginning where we attempt to focus on incorporating the voices and interests of the youth and adult participants, there are several limitations that have impeded our progress. First of all, we often do not have the institutional support (school board, community housing, middle school or university administration) we need in terms of an adequate place to work with students, supplies, uninterrupted time to work, transportation to bring youth to the university campus and other places and collaborative exchanges with content area teachers who work with our youth every day, but who rarely have the time to cooperate with us in our programs. All of these limitations take away from the time we can spend affecting necessary change in institutions that our youth participants bring to our attention. For example, Ernesto has repeatedly expressed concerns about the lack of public transportation in his community, pointing to the ways in which this inhibits youth and others from taking advantage of available public resources such as the university library or the state museum in the down-town areas of our city. In answer to this concern, we have written multiple letters to city authorities but have not been successful yet in developing robust partner-ships with the city and schools that would support sustainable changes.

Most importantly, in terms of our work with youth, we also feel we need to include more intentionally a reflective component in our work, a place and time where youth and adults think not only of the issues that face them, but also reflect on and learn more about the semiotic resources that they can use to effect change. Unfortunately, due to the frenzied nature of afterschool and summer programs with competing interests, time is always an issue with our youth co-researchers. Thus, although we engage in sequenced modalities, we are limited in having sufficient time to consistently provide and guide deeply reflective processes at the beginning or end of each module that would support youth and pre-service teachers in developing a meta-awareness that would allow them to think more abstractly about the patterns in the semiotic resources they are using. Nor is there often enough time to think about how they could use and manipulate these resources in the various social contexts in which they may find themselves. Research points to the importance of seeing language and literacy development as emerging from language use in authentic contexts and purposes (Halliday, 1978). However, development is enhanced if educators also support youth and their allies in noticing the patterns of language and other semiosis. We still struggle with this second part but believe that in time, our work can expand to also include a focus on collaboratively developing a metalanguage that will more easily support our co-participants in transferring their eloquent play and performance in our work together to other contexts (Schleppegrell, 2013).

Our CS SFL troupe of authors for this book and facilitators of our programs, is a very small one. To challenge the normative practices of schooling and city, we need to move toward very carefully developed partnerships at a local and national level that speak back against the ever-widening gap between impov-erished and wealthy neighborhoods and schools. The Yamacraw program in Savannah attests to the power of longitudinal work that involves city, school and community members. It also provides for us a pronounced sense that the only way this work happens is if we have the requisite resources from public and private sources, to properly fund staff to do the work. Community and politi-cal buy-in are vital and they can only be built with cultural insiders in concert with content experts. In many cases we have found, those identities will overlap, although this isn't always true. For our work to be successful in the long run, we need to keep getting up and building new relationships with others outside of our immediate zone, relationships that support us in responding to the visions, fears and needs of our youth and adult participants.

Implications

Our book highlights how we see resource pedagogies such as CS SFL praxis as pivotal approaches to challenge the current racist and anti-immigration discourses that inform institutional practices. By entering and owning culturally sustaining spaces where diverse languages, everyday lived experiences and register switching co-construct understandings of community and disciplinary knowledge, minoritized youth may get to see themselves as dynamic civic change agents, ready to speak back to social inequity. In a recent workshop at Chestnut Middle School, one young boy responded to a question about what he had valued about a drama workshop by saying, "I learned that we can have opinions too." Chilling as this may seem, the fact that a 14-year-old boy feels he is not entitled to have opinions in school spaces points to the necessity of CS SFL praxis in supporting youth to convey their civic agency. It can provide a third space in which adolescents can come to see and understand that they not only do have a voice but that their voice is valued and needed. Edgar who has worked in our CS SFL programs for the past four years and now serves as a leader in our programs, described his routine daily life as one of incarceration because of the lack of affordable public transportation and youth spaces. Below is a poem created by Edgar (Chagoya & Harman, 2017) that described how he saw his life at the time as a continual, unexciting loop from *school to home to work; from home to school to work; from work to home* and from there to work that is underpaid.

Caged Dreams
I have been caged all my life
Lost my tears, I couldn't cry
Fighting with all my strife
Trying to reach the sky
The cool refreshing breeze
Makes me feel at ease
Which they just like to tease
That peace I want to please
Five of us in a cage
With not exactly the best wage
Back in my young age
In great games I used to engage
It is the same routine
Always the same scene
I am not afraid to dream
But they seem to disappear (Chagoya & Harman, 2017)

Discussion

As illustrated in this book, a CS SFL praxis can support multilingual youth in interpreting, using and embodying rich multimodal and linguistic repertoires that they already may use in their everyday lives but that are silenced in school contexts. Use of these dynamic repertoires can support disciplinary knowledge generation and civic agency (Pacheco, 2012). Some may argue that our programs are different from regular school practices because our programs are supported by a rich set of resources such as access to adult co-researchers, art educators and community artists. However, we believe that youth program facilitators can develop similar types of relationships with college and community groups willing to participate in civic agency programs that support stronger ties and relationships across age, race and class. Indeed, although our work has been largely in afterschool or summer spaces, the CS SFL approach to knowledge generation in our orchestrated multimodal curriculum also can be used in classroom instruction.

The embodied inquiry and focus on multimodal practices can disrupt the reductive teaching to the test practices that our youth members experience too often in under-resourced school districts. For example, Harman et al (in press) highlight how a CS SFL professional development initiative for science educators and bilingual students supported inclusion of the knowledges, languages and cultures of local student communities. Specifically, multilingual family workshops incorporated the sophisticated linguistic and cultural repertoires of Latine students and family members into the curriculum while making the richness of these resources differently visible to the teachers. For educators interested in developing CS SFL practices, we recommend the following areas of expertise: (1) a working knowledge of SFL and multimodality; (2) an understanding of how to co-construct knowledge with youth in embodied modules that culminate in a project with a broader purpose and audience; (3) an awareness of how multilingualism cultivates a rich dialogic space for adults and youth and (4) an explicit awareness of how dominant language and literacy policies have been used to denigrate the community practices of minoritized youth.

Since the first instantiation of our CS SFL programs, we developed a partnership and community center with residents in an affordable housing complex, guided there by Cierra and Jason Mizell. As a small but dedicated CS SFL troupe, we aim to keep building up a downtown space as a meeting place of hearts, minds and bodies. However, the space/place will always be a contested one. Our memories, our difficult lived experiences, our dreams, our laughter all imbue the center with hauntings from a racialized, inequitable system. Nearby the towers of the highly privileged university building loom over our small cramped community spaces.

References

Abu El-Haj, T. R., & Rubin, B. C. (2009). Realizing the equity-minded aspirations of detracking and inclusion: Toward a capacity-oriented framework for teacher education. *Curriculum Inquiry, 39*(3), 435–463.

Cammarota, J., & Fine, M. (Eds.). (2008). *Revolutionizing education: Youth participatory action research in motion.* New York, NY: Routledge.

Chagoya, E. E., & Harman, R. (2017, April). In lockdown: Where is the joy of our youth? *Journal of Language and Literacy Education.* Retrieved May 4 2018, from http://jolle.coe. uga.edu/wp-content/uploads/2017/04/chagoya_harman.pdf

Collier, D. R., & Rowsell, J. (2014). A room with a view: Revisiting the multiliteracies manifesto, twenty years on. *Fremdsprachen Lehren und Lernen, 43*(2), 12.

Davis, K. (2009). Agentive youth research: Towards individual, collective, and policy transformations. In T. G. Wiley, J. S. Lee, & R. Rumbergers (Eds.) *The education of language minority immigrants in the USA* (pp. 202–239). London, UK: Multilingual Matters.

Derr, V., Chawla, L., & Mintzer, M. (2018). *Placemaking with children and youth: Participatory practices for planning sustainable communities.* New York, NY: New Village Press.

Duncan, G. (2002). Beyond love: A critical race ethnography of the schooling of adolescent black males. *Equity & Excellence in Education, 35*(2), 131–143.

Fisher, M. (2007). *Writing in rhythm: Spoken word in urban classrooms.* New York, NY: Teachers College Press.

Freire, P. (1998). *Teachers as cultural workers: Letters to those who dare to teach* (D. Macedo, D. Koike, & A. Oliveira, Trans.). Boulder, CO: Westview Press.

Ginwright, S. (2008). Collective radical imagination: Youth participatory action research and the art of emancipator knowledge. In J. Cammarota & M. Fine (Eds.) *Revolutionizing education: Youth participatory action research in motion* (pp.13–22). New York and London: Routledge.

Greene, S., Burke, K. J., & McKenna, M. K. (2016). When words fail, art speaks: Learning to listen to youth stories in a community photovoice project. In S. Greene, K. J. Burke, & M. K. McKenna (Eds.) *Youth voices, public spaces, and civic engagement* (pp. 235–258). New York, NY: Routledge.

Halliday, M. A. K. (1978). *Language as social semiotic.* Baltimore, MD: University Park Press.

Harman, R., Buxton, C., Cardozo-Gaibisso, L., Lei, J., & Bui, K (in press). Culturally sustaining praxis in science classrooms. *Language and Education*

Harman, R., Siffrinn, N., Mizell, J., & Bui, K. (in press). Promoting reflection literacy in pre-service language teacher education: Critical SFL praxis with multilingual youth. In L. Altariste & C. Crosby (Eds.) *Second language writing across PK16 contexts: Intersections of teaching, learning, and development.* Ann Arbor, MI: University of Michigan Press.

Heath, S. B. (2015). Creativity and the work of art and science: A cognitive neuroscience perspective. In M. Fleming, L. Bresler, & J. O'Toole (Eds.) *The Routledge International Handbook of the Arts and Education* (pp. 398–409). New York, NY: Routledge.

Heath, S. B. (2018). The Arts as Brick and Mortar of Community Building. Aralee Strange Speaker Series, Georgia Museum of Art.

Humphrey, S. (2008). *Adolescent literacies for critical social and community engagement.* Unpublished dissertation, University of New England, Australia.

Humphrey, S. (2010). 'Modelling social affiliation and genre in the civic domain'. In A. Mahboob & N. Knight (Eds.) *Appliable linguistics* (pp. 76–91). London, England: Continuum.

Kim, R. H. (2013). 'Never knew literacy could get at my soul': On how words matter for youth, or notes toward decolonizing literacy. *Review of Education, Pedagogy, and Cultural Studies, 35*(5), 392–407.

Kinloch, V. (2010). *Harlem on our minds: Place, race, and the literacies of urban youth.* New York, NY: Teachers College Press.

Kirkland, D. E. (2004). Rewriting school: Critical pedagogy in the writing classroom. *Journal of Teaching Writing, 21,* 83–96.

Kirshner, B. (2010). Productive tensions in youth participatory action research. *National Society for the Study of Education, 109*(1), 238–251.

Kirshner, B., & Jefferson, A. (2015). Participatory democracy and struggling schools: Making space for youth in school turnaround. *Teachers College Record, 117*(6), 1–26.

Lee, C. (2007). *Culture, literacy, and learning: Taking bloom in the midst of the whirlwind.* New York, NY: Teachers College Press.

Lukin, A., Moore, A. R., Herke, M., Wegener, R., & Wu, C. (2011). Halliday's model of register revisited and explored. *Linguistics and the Human Sciences, 4*(2), 187–213.

Mitra, D. L. (2009). The role of intermediary organizations in sustaining student voice initiatives. *Teachers College Record, 111*(7), 1834–1868.

North, C. E. (2008). What is all this talk about 'social justice'? Mapping the terrain of education's latest catchphrase. *Teachers College Record, 110*(6), 1182–1206.

Pacheco, M. (2012). Learning in/through everyday resistance: A cultural-historical perspective on community resources and curriculum. *Educational Researcher, 41*(4), 121–132.

Paris, D., & Alim, H. S. (2014). What are we seeking to sustain through culturally sustaining pedagogy? A loving critique forward. *Harvard Educational Review, 84(1),* 85–100.

Potts, D., & Moran, M. J. (2013). Mediating multilingual children's language resources. *Language and Education, 27*(5), 451–468.

Rosenfeld Halverson, E. (2010). Film as identity exploration: A multimodal analysis of youth-produced films. *Teachers College Record, 112*(9), 2352–2378.

Rubin, B. C., Abu El-Haj, T. R., Graham, E., & Clay, K. (2016). Confronting the urban civic opportunity gap: Integrating youth participatory action research into teacher education. *Journal of Teacher Education, 67*(5), 424–436.

Schleppegrell, M. (2013). The role of meta-language in supporting academic language development. *Language Learning, 63*(1), 153–170.

Siffrinn, N., & Harman, R. (2019). Toward an embodied systemic functional linguistics. *TESOL Quarterly.* Retrieved December 10, 2019, from https://doi.org/10.1002/tesq.516

INDEX

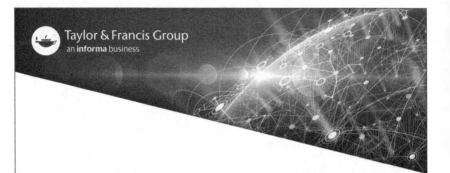

Printed in the United States
by Baker & Taylor Publisher Services

•